Exceptionally Human

Successful Communication in a Distracted World

Exceptionally Human

Successful Communication in a Distracted World

Brian Shapiro

Shapiro Communications Publishing
2016

First Printing: 2016

ISBN: 978-0-9972848-0-5

Shapiro Communications Publishing
245 S. 16th Street
Philadelphia, PA 19102

www.shapirocommunications.com

Acknowledgments

First and foremost, I would like to thank all the current and former clients Shapiro Communications has had the pleasure to work with. Without your trust in us and belief in exceptionally human communication, our ability to positively contribute to your organizations' communication success would not have occurred. I would like to thank Peter McEllhenney and John Cipollone at Endgame. As Exceptionally Human's copy editor, Peter's adept eye and keen understanding allowed this project to fully take flight. And John's unending and humorous honesty proved inspiring to getting this project off the ground. I would also like to thank Phylinda Moore for her outstanding final editing, Greg Thomas for the cover design, Bijan Yashar for the cover photo, and Nicki Toizer for her layout design. Thanks to Alan Barstow at The University of Pennsylvania's Organizational Dynamics program, for the opportunity to bring valuable communication content to the curriculum. Special thanks goes out to Danette Wilson, who has faithfully supported Shapiro Communications since relocating to Philadelphia in 2011. Her unwavering support and efforts have allowed us to traverse some challenging times and flourish.

I would also like to thank the city of Philadelphia, a vibrant city whose embrace has proven warm and welcoming, and a place with far, far more to offer than food stereotypes and fictional boxers. Thank you to the Greater Philadelphia Chamber of Commerce, for providing thoughtful networking and connection opportunities. Special thanks to Center City Proprietors Association, an organization that provides a true sense of community, as well as the Philadelphia Society for People and Strategy, for the marvelous professional education programs they provide that keep thinking and practice on the cutting edge. And thank you to San Francisco, my former home for 20 years and where Shapiro Communications was launched.

Finally, I would like to thank my family for their patience throughout this writing process. To my wife, Adina, who has been quite tolerant of some stress-induced, less-than-exceptional communication on my part, thank you. Her understanding served as a continual reminder that talking about exceptional communication is the easy part, and practicing it requires just that. And to my young sons, Asa and Levi, who lovingly challenge my ability to communicate effectively, patiently, and thoughtfully, while reflecting back to me how valuable being exceptionally human is.

Table of Contents

Chapter 1

Exceptionally Human

"Try not to think of anything as a problem. Start with a forgiving relationship to laziness and impatience and cultivate a sense of humor about them both. And then trick them."
–Anne Bogart, A Director Prepares

It was almost preordained that I would wind up having a career in Communication. Having grown up in the Land of Oz, or what is otherwise known as Los Angeles, in a music industry family, I witnessed first-hand how communication generated and created fantastic realities. A pulling of levers here, some smoke blown there, and *voilà*, a star was born...or not. More often than not it was the ability to spin, or better yet, to persuade, that allowed one person to get the recording contract and the other to keep his or her day job. Sure, talent played a significant role, but it was how that talent was packaged and displayed that made the final difference.

I had a front-row seat to these spin-persuasion sessions. I had the opportunity to experience the wizards in action, watch people become spellbound, and see what stuck and what fell by the wayside. I saw how credibility was lost and gained, how powerful emotions were elicited, and how at times perverse logic was swallowed up like little chocolate treats. Little did I know I was privy to the power of communication and the ability to master it, creating the realities in which others live. And it wasn't until I left Los Angeles for college, and started studying communication, and was introduced to Aristotle, that I started to understand that what I had been witnessing, has been taking place for millennia, and that it is *exceptionally human.*

As humans, we all have exceptional qualities. I use the words exceptionally human to highlight those aspects of our behavior that rise above

> *As humans, we all have exceptional qualities.*

and beyond the typical, usual, or standard. Some of us are exceptional in mathematics, or the sciences, or in athletics, and still others in the performing arts, or in music, or the visual arts. Some of us are exceptional spouses, parents, sisters, brothers, and friends. When I say that what I witnessed growing up was exceptionally human, I am referring specifically to a person's ability to master a complex set of skills so as to assure that whatever it is they are communicating is paid attention to, and perhaps most importantly, listened to. Exceptionally human communicators apply time-honored techniques in what appears to be effortless, yet is done in a highly strategic, manner. Exceptionally human communicators recognize and understand what behaviors and words to employ, under what circumstances, and actually have the ability to pull it off. It may not be every time they communicate, but when the need arises, they are at the ready. And soon enough, that will be you as well.

Aristotle was an exceptional human being. Among his many great achievements are his rhetorical proofs, or what I think of as the three elements of exceptional human communication. According to Aristotle, there is *ethos*, the credibility you have and the trust you earn from people. Next, there is *pathos*, the emotions you generate in others. And finally there is *logos*, how reasonable people find your message based on the ideas, facts, and arguments you present. Trust, feeling, and reason are the three qualities Aristotle says we need to persuade people to take action, and the men and women who master these qualities enjoy extraordinary success.

It is a tribute to the strength of Aristotle's insights that more than 2300 years after his death, *ethos* (trust), *pathos* (emotion), and *logos* (reason) are still the foundation of exceptionally human communication and the good results we hope to achieve from our interactions.

I think a lot about Aristotle's three elements. I think about them as a husband and the father of two young children. Marriage and children challenge your communication skills every day! I think about them as a business consultant whose job it is to help organizations, through their communication and interpersonal interactions, create exceptionally positive outcomes for their people, their customers and their clients. More often than not, I think about them most when I interact with businesses as a customer myself, or when I think back to those times when I was an employee.

Probably because one aspect of my work is focused on helping businesses create satisfying interactions with their clients and customers, I also tend to focus on whether businesses create satisfying interactions with me. This is another way of saying I have high expectations. Or maybe what I really mean is I can be that guy who is a real pain in the butt. I try not to be that guy. But despite my 20+ years of yoga and tai chi practice, my moods vary widely and so my reactions to businesses vary as well. Sometimes I am quite forgiving of oversights, missed appointments, defective products, and inattentive if not outright indifferent service. Other times my tolerance for these things sit at near zero and I almost instantaneously feel that surge of energy that comes right before an unpleasant outburst. I am not proud of myself when I lose my temper but I'm human. I have my good and bad days, and I don't like it when expectations fall short, when people fail to live up to their word or the promised deadlines are not met, especially as a customer or client.

Because I have a fair amount of experience being "that guy" I can tell you Aristotle's three elements, *ethos*, *pathos*, and *logos*, have a huge influence on how I react. People who earn my trust, who I view as credible, who are aware of what feelings are being generated, and offer a reasonable explanation, will not make me angry even when I am having the worst of days. These folks might tell me about a problem – about something that should make me angry – but it doesn't because the manner in which they have communicated exercised the best of what Aristotle's three elements offer. On the other hand, people who do little or none of the things Aristotle recommends can make me furious on the best of days. Even when the product or service involved in the transaction was suitable. I think of this as "the meal was delicious but the waiter was a jerk" problem.

Here's a good example of exceptionally human communication being the difference maker. It comes from our neighborhood parents' listserv, which serves as a forum for anything from parenting challenges to assorted home-related advice. There are 2 cable/internet providers that serve our neighborhood, and in this exchange, one parent is trying to determine if switching cable/internet providers is worth the effort. Here's the exchange (the company names have been made generic):

Parent 1: Has anyone else been talked into switching to Cable Company A in the neighborhood? There's a nice sales guy who is winning me over. Is it worth it? He says other people are doing it. I'm wondering if it's true!

Parent 2: We have it. It's fine. Cable Company A is really no better than Cable Company B. You have to use their cable modem which has a built in router that has terrible Wi-Fi penetration in our 3 story row home - but I hear Cable Company B has the same modem/router setup as well now so I doubt it's much different.

Parent 1: Well, I'm doing it. Will let you all know how it compares!

Note the determining factor here. It was NOT the service itself, but rather "the nice sales guy." Clearly, this nice sales guy was fairly exceptional, for when Parent 1 went to seek out additional information and what they received basically said both providers were the same, it was the nice sales guy who made the difference. Let that be a lesson for us all. The *ethos* was not too high for either provider and the *logos* was the same, but the *ethos* was the difference maker, as the sales guy was able to elicit positive emotions.

Ethos, pathos and *logos* are so powerful that they can persuade us to become loyal customers of a company that has caused us a problem. They can also persuade us to never step foot again in a business that hasn't caused us a problem. According to Bruce Temkin, Managing Partner of Temkin

> *Ethos, pathos and logos are so powerful that they can persuade us to become loyal customers of a company that has caused us a problem.*

Group, a customer service research and consulting firm, "When companies responded very poorly after a bad experience, 47% of consumers stopped spending completely with the company. When they had a very good response, only 6% stopped spending and 37% increased their spending... Consumers that are satisfied with customer service interactions are 4x's more likely to repurchase than those who are dissatisfied." So a good question to ask is what defines satisfaction, and my answer would be found in *ethos, pathos,* and *logos.*

The purpose of this book then is to help you use Aristotle's insights to be more successful in your professional life, and find additional success in your community and personal relationships. To that end, I would like to say first that *you are already a good communicator*. We naturally communicate well with the spouses, partners, family, friends, co-workers, and customers in our lives. Otherwise, we wouldn't have been able to develop relationships with them. So the goal is not to get you to be a good communicator, but rather to help you become an exceptionally human communicator. I want you to become a Nobel Prize winning communicator, an undisputed National Champion communicator, a poster child for communication, or to put it quite simply, to become the best possible communicator a person can be. I want you to be *Exceptionally Human!*

Now, I feel it is important to say that is probably, at the very least, an overly ambitious goal. My goodness, professional baseball players are considered highly successful when they fail to get a hit 7 out of 10 times, and in basketball missing 5 out of 10 shots is equally impressive. We are all human and that means we are all less than perfect, and will be less than perfect. Nobody will be the best communicator at all times, myself included. However, we can all continually get better and improve our chances of having more successful interactions, and as a result, more positive outcomes. Aim high! Aim higher than you might have previously imagined or thought possible, so that although you may not hit the mark every time, your overall performance will be that much more improved.

12 minutes in the morning, 12 minutes in the afternoon, that's all

In other words, I want to increase the probability that your communication will be outstanding. All I'm asking for is a modest 5% improvement, or focused effort, in your communication effectiveness. In a typical 40-hour workweek, 5% equals only 24 total minutes a day. A 5% focused effort, 12 minutes in the morning, and 12 minutes in the afternoon, can produce remarkable results, especially if that 5% is compounded, which it will be if you constantly strive for that 5%. There is no end point, only continual and regular improvement, and with it, continual and regular results.

Let me tell you how I would like us to do this. First, I would like to talk about how communication actually works. I am going to dip into my graduate studies, but I promise this discussion won't be dry or academic or dull. There are fascinating insights from communication studies research that are simple to understand and that have incredibly powerful possibilities when applied in our everyday work lives.

You are going to hear me talk about two of these insights a lot. They are **perception** and **lack of control**. When we communicate, our message is what the other person perceives it to be and not necessarily what we intended. We all know how it feels to be misunder-

9

stood. We also lose control over our message the moment we speak it or send it. Then our message falls under the control of the person who receives it and sometimes we are really surprised by what they do with that message.

Next, we will talk about **communication competence** and our communication styles. What are our preferred modes of communicating with other people and what are the outcomes of those styles? We will also talk about adapting our communication style to the preferred style of the person receiving our message. Exceptionally human communicators can spot the different communication styles of people and adapt their interactions from person to person, while still maintaining their integrity. This isn't always easy to do but when we do it right, the results can be phenomenal.

We will also take a more in-depth look at Aristotle's three rhetorical proofs, or his three elements: *ethos* (trust), *pathos* (emotion) and *logos* (reason). Yes, we're going to dip into some good old Greek philosophy, but in a fun, highly relevant manner. We are going to talk about how you can use these proven communications techniques to become more adept at the three elements. These tips are most certainly acquirable, and although it does take some focused effort to learn them, they can and will make an immediate and powerful difference in how well you communicate. We will break each element down, and guide you towards mastering each one of them. Most importantly, we will provide some guidance as to where you can locate the places in your organization where having exceptionally human communication can make a real difference, places I like to refer to as **key organizational interactions**.

Throughout the book, we will talk about using different communication mediums, especially the newer electronic ones like email and social media. Digital communication tools are powerful but they come with special pitfalls. We will look at how to avoid the pitfalls and harness that power. Another change is the rise of "outstanding service" as the key

> *Digital communication tools are powerful but they come with special pitfalls.*

value that differentiates one business from another and especially a business that succeeds from a business that fails. We now live in a world where anybody can do business with anybody, anywhere around the globe at any time. It is hard to compete on price today. The best price is one Google search on our smartphones away. It is hard to compete on product. Anything you can buy in a store you can buy online, from one of dozens of companies, and have shipped right to you.

We will finish up by reinforcing why *ethos*, *pathos*, and *logos* are even more important to our professional success, the success of the businesses we own, or work for than ever before. They can teach us to become *exceptionally human* communicators to thrive in today's world. And unlike the blurry world that is Hollywood, where Aristotle's tools are often used in a dicey, hit or miss way, you can approach every interaction with integrity, have it received and perceived in the way you intended, and become an *exceptionally human communicator*. So, without further ado, let's begin!

Chapter 2

Communication: Simple and Straight-Forward

"I found that when I wrote a very sad piece people were as apt to laugh as they were to be moved. So I gave up the notion of communication as impractical in my case."
–John Cage

Here is something worth taking into serious consideration, however distressing it may be: You have precious little control of your communication. Hold on! How is that possible? In the last chapter, we agreed that all of us are pretty decent communicators, which means we must have some control over our messages, even after we send them, right? Well, sort of. There's an old axiom in the field of communication studies that says you cannot not communicate, that we are always communicating, whether we like it or not. That means that people are continually interpreting and ascribing meaning to our actions and behaviors. That leads into

another axiom, which is once the message you are trying to communicate has left your body, be it written,
verbal, or otherwise, you have in essence lost all control
over its meaning. The control over the message's meaning now belongs to the person/people you delivered it
to. And their interpretation of the meaning may have
very little to do with the actual content of your message. People can ascribe meaning to just about anything
you do or don't do. So the extent of control you have
over your message is actually quite limited.

Think about the countless times in our personal
and professional life that we have carefully crafted
the most accurate message possible, only to have the
other person interpret it in a way that was quite different than what we intended. It happens every day.
The problem, this lack of control I refer to, comes from
the place I call the **interpretive gap**. Interpretive gaps
are those spaces between how we intend a message to
be received and the mean-
ing other people give to that
message, the "filling in the
blanks", so to speak. People
interpret! People fill in the
blanks! And more often than
not, people fill in the blanks
as they want to, or as they
desire, not as we hope they

> *Interpretive gaps are those spaces between how we intend a message to be received and the meaning other people give to that message...*

will. Simply put, all our communication is at the mercy of those around us and we are dependent on their accurate interpretation in order to have quality communication. One of my first goals for us in this book is to help reduce the interpretive gaps people fill in when we communicate and as a result, increase the chances for understanding. To do this, let me talk briefly about what communication is and how it works. And after that, I will reveal what we need to do to keep those interpretive gaps as narrow as possible.

What Communication Is (And Is Not)

When we think of communication, we may think about talking to friends and family, sending a text or email, talking on the phone, or reading a book, magazine or newspaper. TV shows and movies are also communication, as is the sharing of photos and videos. But for better or worse, communication is also something we absolutely take for granted. We think it is natural to take ideas and feelings that exist solely inside ourselves and communicate them in such a way that people understand them the same way that we do. We forget how truly remarkable our ability to communicate really is. How it works is remarkable too.

For simplicity's sake, let's say communication is something that occurs between two people: **the sender** and **the receiver**. The sender wants to take thoughts she has in her head (and/or feelings she has in her body) and express them so the receiver understands exactly what she is thinking and feeling. To do this, the sender must use **symbols**.

What are symbols? Definitively speaking, symbols are representations of something else. The words you are reading right now are symbols that represent ideas. Facial expressions are symbols that represent how we are feeling. Think of the Stars and Stripes as being a symbolic representation of the United States, or any other nation's flag as being a symbolic representation of that nation. Symbols evoke thoughts and feelings in people who share a common understanding of what these symbols mean and when they share the same meaning, they increase their chances of understanding each other. As humans, the most common symbol we use is language, and according to Ethnologue, worldwide there are over 7,000 actively used languages. It is through language that we attempt to communicate what we think and feel, and apparently in 7,000 distinct ways!

Once our thoughts and feelings are symbolized, we have a **message**. This message is transmitted from the sender to the receiver through what is called the channel or medium. A medium can be verbal, it can be written, and in the digital age it can be posting photos and videos. The **message** represents – and the key word here is r_e_p_r_e_s_e_n_t_s– what the sender is thinking and feeling. Our hope is that the receiver interprets the message in such a way that understanding is achieved. It's a lofty goal, and in reality, we do a fairly good job of it.

Yet, this rather simple way of looking at communication presents many challenges. The first of these challenges is the assumption. The assumption is our expectation that the other person will interpret what we express in the way we intended, that the other person will know exactly what we mean when we make a statement, or write an email, or post a photo. The problem is that all symbols are subject to interpretation, those interpretive gaps I referred to, those "filling in of the blanks" we talked about a little earlier, and with every symbol exchanged between people, the interpretive gap between what we intended to communicate and how it is received can be wide.

Sometimes that gap is quite large, such as someone making eye contact with you across a crowded room. Do they like you? Do they know you? Are they even looking at you? What are the many things that look could mean? Other times the gap is very narrow, such as when someone says, "You are a dear friend" in a sincere voice. But if said in a sarcastic voice, the gap opens wider. When an advertisement promises "the best in the region!" the interpretive gap can be so wide we can't see across it with binoculars. When we get a lawyer to review a contract that guarantees our satisfaction, there should be no gap at all.

So, really, it is the receiver who ultimately controls the meaning of our communication. This is another way of saying that our messages are what our receivers perceive them to be and that perception is another key idea in communications studies we really need to talk about. To explain this idea further, let me tell you a story:

On The Jet Way

As many people know, the winter of 2015 was a frigid one on the East Coast. For 2 days, I got a reprieve when I traveled to visit family back in Los Angeles where temperatures were in the low 60s. As I prepared to board my return flight back to Philadelphia, I stood in line on the jet way.

Given the flight, like most flights nowadays, was completely full, people were required to check their carry-on roller bags. Standing at the lower end of the jet way were 2 baggage handlers who were going to take all the bags into the plane's belly. People were grumpy, not only because they had to check their would-be carry-on bags, but because they were leaving balmy Southern California and returning to winter. It was snowing/sleeting back in Philadelphia on this March day. One of the baggage handlers, in a rather sarcastic and somewhat condescending tone, began to address the long line of people waiting to get on the airplane.

"What in the world do all you people want to go back to Philadelphia for? Look at it outside here, it's a little cloudy but it's breaking up and the sun is coming out and it's nice and warm. I don't understand it."

Wait a second! Did this guy just say that? I'm originally from Los Angeles, and although I've adapted to winter, come March I much prefer warmth to cold. Not only that, I paid over $600 to make this trip on a crowded airplane. And now I'm being taunted… What gives? And it was pretty clear from the expression on the faces of everyone around me, that his improvised outburst was not appreciated.

As the line slowly marched forward, I wound up next to the guy. I asked him what he was thinking, having a little fun at the customers' expense. He said he was only kidding around by trying to inject a little humor, and the manner in which he expressed that to me led me to truly believe him. I mentioned what he said, and the way he said it, could easily be taken the wrong way given the circumstances (grumpy people getting ready to get on a packed plane heading towards the freezer). He concurred. We had a little laugh as I boarded the plane and he took the bags down below. I was fine as I'd had additional communication to close the interpretive gap, but who knows how other people felt. Perhaps they were pissed. Perhaps they were offended. Perhaps they didn't care. But all of them came to interpret the man's message in the way they perceived it, not necessarily the way he intended. Oh my.

The Foundations of World Class Communication-Communication Competence

So the big challenges standing between us and our goal of becoming exceptionally human, World Class, and undisputed National Champion communicators are lack of control, or the interpretive gaps, and the receiver's perception. When I say World Class, undisputed National Champion communicators, I mean being able to produce desired outcomes through our communication. An important strategy in generating desired outcomes is becoming a competent communicator, or what is known as Brian Spitzberg and William Cupach's theory of **communication competence**.

Roughly defined, communication competence is when the manner in which a message is communicated is acceptable to both parties, NOT the content. Or, it's not what you say but how you say it that makes you competent. Being a competent communicator means you have the ability to craft and deliver your message in such a way that the person or people you are sending it to will find the crafting and delivery acceptable, even if they disagree with or find the content upsetting. An exceptionally human communicator expresses herself in a manner that is acceptable to both herself and her receiver. It's really

> *Being a competent communicator means you have the ability to craft and deliver your message in such a way that the person or people you are sending it to will find the crafting and delivery acceptable...*

the ability to keep other people positively engaged with us.

The truth is communication competence takes lots of hard work and practice, as we are not born competent communicators. As infants, we really only have one effective way in which we convey messages, crying. If we were hungry, tired, had a soggy diaper, or simply needed to be held, we cried. To those without children, all crying may seem alike. I can tell you from first-hand experience, it is not. After our oldest son was born, we found our apartment not only filled with new love and joy, but plenty of crying. Over the course of those first weeks and months, my wife and I began to notice subtle variations in our son's crying that would inform us what he was trying to express. For instance, when he had short little bleating cries, he was hungry. When he cried with an extended whine, his diaper needed changing. And there were many times when he cried and we had absolutely no idea what he was trying to express (in all honestly, this was more often than not). However, making the distinctions between his various cries, helped us give him what he needed, and bring a temporary peace to our home, however short-lived. At the same time, the rest of the world is not our parents, nor should it be, so this is an exception to the rule.

Fortunately, as we grow up, we gain access to language and can begin to explicitly express our needs, and that's when we take the first steps to become competent communicators. And at the same time, many of our fellow humans will simply find crying out for their needs is the best approach they have to getting their needs met. I think you know what I'm talking about here, but just in case you don't, let me put it more directly: some people will whaa whaa whaa their way through life, without any attempts whatsoever at becoming competent communicators. Bottom line, competence is a LEARNED behavior, one that requires practice, experimentation, failure, discipline, and determination. The effort may seem rather significant, but the payoff is well worth the time invested.

What makes a competent communicator? It starts

with recognizing there is **no one ideal way to communicate**. What works in one situation will not necessarily work in another. It may be perfectly acceptable to use sharp language and a direct manner with one person, but it may totally backfire with another. So, first and foremost, a competent communicator must **develop a large repertoire of communication styles**. That means for those of

> *What works in one situation will not necessarily work in another.*

us who prefer using more direct and assertive communication approaches, we must begin to develop alternative approaches, and vice versa. We must begin to take ourselves out of our communication comfort zones and start using methods, styles, and approaches that although they may be initially uncomfortable, over time will produce positive outcomes and become integrated into our overall communication efforts.

A classic difference between communications styles is the difference between East Coast and West Coast in the United States. As a person who grew up in Los Angeles, spent 20 years in San Francisco, a couple short stints in New York City, and now lives in Philadelphia, I can tell you the difference is real. On the East Coast, people tend to be more direct and in the cities, this directness can be accompanied with a hard tone. On the West Coast, people are less direct. They can be leisurely in getting to the point. One is not better than the other, just simply different. For someone from the East Coast, West Coasters can seem rambling, aloof and wordy. For someone from the West Coast, East Coasters can seem blunt and rude. As I've spent more years on the East Coast, my communication has become more direct and to the point. So, when I return to the West Coast, as I often do, my communication can take people aback, that is until I adjust and return to my West Coast ways. This adjusting is my attempt at becoming a competent communicator.

Second, where is this communication taking place? In other words, **what is the context?** Every setting has its own implicit and explicit set of rules, and we want to clearly understand what those rules are to avoid any unintentional violation. Context is what grounds all communication, and allows mutual meaning to be achieved. It is the frame around which the communication is placed. If what is being communicated is done so absent of context, then all bets are off, and achieving mutually satisfying communication is left to chance. One behaves rather differently on a job interview than they would when hanging out with close friends, or they would in a sales situation, or during a performance review. Context rules, figuratively and literally, and we must know the rules to know what is acceptable and what is not.

Finally, consideration must be given to the following two questions. **What is our goal?** And **what is our relationship with the other person?** For instance, if we have a dispute we wish to resolve with a neighbor, we may take a more congenial communication approach to resolve the matter, as this person lives next to us, so we want to keep things on good terms as a result. However, if our dispute is with a person at a company in another state or country that we don't intend to do business with again, we may be more direct or aggressive, as our relationship with them is far more distant and the chances we'll need something from them in the future is rather limited.

Empathy also plays a key role in competent communication. Feeling what another person is feeling, or attempting to understand how they might feel, will help inform our communication choices. If I anticipate the person may get upset with the information being delivered, I may try to deliver it in such a way that at least doesn't compound the upset. Empathy goes a long way in avoiding unnecessary messiness in communication, because if you can anticipate how a receiver may emotionally respond to you, you can make choices so as to bring about a more desirable emotional response.

Here's a good example. The other night, my wife and I had one of our coveted date nights. The kids were with the grandparents and we had a night to

25

ourselves. We decided to see a film, and centered our evening around the screening time. We planned to have a relaxing dinner prior, but as we kicked-back in our temporarily responsibility-less, childfree home, we lost track of time and suddenly movie-time was closing in. Because of this, a relaxing sit-down dinner became impossible, so we grabbed a quick bite, hurriedly ate, then hailed a cab to the movie theater. Upon arriving at the theater, utility trucks were everywhere and two people in beach chairs were camped in front of the theater entrance. We were informed that the theater was closed, due to an underground utility fire that had left several blocks power-free for two days.

As you might imagine, we weren't thrilled. The theater website had no notice of the closing. Had we known ahead of time, we would have planned things differently. But, such is life. And as you also might imagine, these two folks informing people of the theater's closing weren't thrilled either, having to repeat the same story to countless disappointed people for the past two days. This was hardly a win-win situation.

I asked the folks why the information wasn't on the website. My question was met with a shrug. We were told we could go to another theater, close by that would be showing the same film 1½ hours later. We mentioned that would be too late for us. "Bummer" one of them replied. Bummer? Bummer? We walked away not only disappointed, but a little pissed-off as well.

Yes, bummer indeed. Bummer for us, as we infrequently have a night to ourselves and we scheduled this one around something that wasn't even going to happen. Bummer for those guys, who had to deal with disappointed person after person. Bummer for the businesses who were losing out on profits because of something outside of their control. Bummers all around.

In spite of the bummers, there had been a way to handle this situation in a more exceptionally human way that would've minimize the annoyance, or at least not have amplified it for the customer. Many times, it's not necessarily the resolution of a problem that matters, but how one handles the inability to resolve the problem. Saying, "Bummer," was like saying, "Too bad," or "That's life." Now, those things may be true, but they don't help the situation, they exacerbate it. Such a response doesn't make someone want to do business with that entity again. A better way for business to communicate is to acknowledge the person's "bummer" and to express empathy for their disappointment. Doing so won't resolve the situation, but it won't create an opportunity for someone to take his or her frustra-

> *A better way for business to communicate is to acknowledge the person's "bummer" and to express empathy for their disappointment.*

tion and disappointment out on you and your business...because that would really be a bummer. In fact,
expressing empathy can lead to increased customer
loyalty. That's an exceptionally human insight.

Achieving competence requires repeated practice
and effort. But it is worth it in the long run, as it will
allow you to create greater and more meaningful connections with a wider range of people. For anyone
learning how to play chess, one of the first lessons is to
look a few moves ahead before moving. Communication researchers Brant Burleson and Scott Caplan refer
to this quality as **cognitive complexity**. And in our
communication practices, this generally means consciously recognizing what potential consequences are
associated with our communication choices. In working
to understand the possible outcomes to our communication style, we will better inform ourselves as to what
is necessary to become a competent communicator. It
does require us to go outside of our comfort zone, to try
something new, and face failure. We will not get it right
every time, but over time, we'll get it right more often
than not, and that can make a huge difference.

It is easy to think of many examples where being a
competent communicator would have made our lives
better. We have all had arguments with spouses, partners, family members, friends, or business colleagues
that we regret. Most of the time, we probably don't

regret that we addressed the issue at the heart of the argument. We just don't like that we argued about it. We wish we had been kinder, more patient, more understanding, and more respectful. We wish we could have expressed ourselves in a different way. We wish we had listened better and had been listened to better. We wish we had been able to discuss the issue without arguing. It is human for people to disagree, especially when they are disagreeing on things that are important to them. Competent communicators can disagree with people and still make them feel good, and that's what being exceptionally human is all about.

Disagreements happen all the time. In fact, disagreements and conflict are built into the heart and bones and muscles of being human. I firmly believe, however, and I know I'm not alone, that success in business comes from good relationships more than anything else and exceptionally human communicators are superb at negotiating, proposing, selling, persuading, and disagreeing with business colleagues WHILE maintaining their relationships with them. To this end, there are a lot of practical communication techniques that, although they take effort, are easy to learn and use and can help you become that undisputed National Champion, poster child, exceptionally human communicator. And that takes us right back to our good friend, Aristotle.

Exceptionally Human

Chapter 3

The Big Three, Courtesy of Aristotle

"I know of only two other figures besides Aristotle who are equally revered in Western and Islamic traditions; Moses and Jesus. Now that tells you something about the company Aristotle keeps." –Anonymous

If you take the time to consider those people who have had the ability to most influence you, a few things should come to mind. First, they are typically people you perceive as credible, or you trust. Second, they are probably people, who when you think of them, elicit more positive emotions than negative ones. In other words, you generally feel good when they come to mind. Finally, when they are communicating with you, you'll more often than not perceive their communication to be clear, reasonable, and rational. Aristotle's *ethos*, *pathos*, and *logos* is the remarkable combination that will keep us engaged with other people, or if perceived negatively, will push them away. Once again, exceptionally human communication boils down to how *ethos* (trust), *pathos* (emotion), and *logos* (reason) are perceived, and this is where Aristotle returns to center stage.

Most people are familiar with Aristotle, if not intimately, by name alone. As a little refresher, Aristotle was an ancient Greek (actually Macedonian) philosopher who wielded great influence not only in Greece, but also across the world. He is one of the few human figures equally revered in the Western and Islamic traditions. In addition to being a philosopher, Aristotle was a biologist, physician, and overall human wonder. He had an amazing ability to remain in uncertain or highly ambiguous situations for prolonged periods of time without giving in to the burning desire to form a logical or reasonable explanation as to what was unfolding around him. This negative capability, as the poet John Keats termed it, is what allowed Aristotle to be such an amazing and insightful observer of animal behavior. In his capacity as a biologist, he made detailed discoveries about animals that, in some cases, were not confirmed by science until several centuries later. And it is because of this ability to observe and understand feral animal behavior, when time came to turn his attention to another animal's behavior, the human being, his observations and conclusions were equally remarkable, and still are as relevant today as they were

23 centuries ago.

Aristotle observed that for one human to persuade another human, 3 essentials are required. Roughly translated, Aristotle discovered what I like to refer to as the instinctual cues we need to provide our fellow human beings so they will strongly consider what we request of them. These 3 essentials are known as Aristotle's Rhetorical Proofs, and as mentioned in the introduction, they are *ethos*, *pathos*, and *logos* — or trust, feeling, and reason. *Ethos* refers to your credibility, or how much trust that you have earned in others. *Pathos* refers to the emotional response, or feelings generated in the person you are communicating with. Finally, *logos* refers to how reasonable, rational, and logical the other person finds your position, request, or argument to be. *Ethos*, *pathos*, and *logos* are perhaps the most significant and powerful insights into human behavior that have ever been made. The person able to master these three elements can essentially get people to do as they would like them to do, in an almost instinctual animal-like way. Now that's power.

I bring Aristotle's Rhetorical Proofs to your attention because first and foremost, they are exceptionally human. As you might imagine, this power has been used for better and for worse throughout human history. Our goal, of course, is to use this power to better our communication practices, so it's essential to keep in mind that these 3 essentials are fluid at all times and under all conditions. Credibility can take years to earn and take only seconds to lose, and just because we've established initial credibility does not mean we will remain credible over time. The same holds true for emotions and logic, as feelings are fleeting, and logic applied to one situation will not necessarily translate to another setting. If the logic we provide is suspect, our credibility can suffer, or if your communication causes someone to feel anxious or nervous, then your logic may not be seen as sound. In other words, Aristotle's Rhetorical Proofs don't exist in separate compartments; they are interrelated, interconnected, and utterly dependent on each other. So let's take some time now to fully grasp the significance of Aristotle's insights so our communication can become that much more exceptionally human.

This is my please don't try to understand us story: My wife and I had recently hired a designer to assist us with a home project. The designer initially met with us and thoughtfully asked us questions as to why we wanted what we wanted and what we hoped the final result would look and feel like. We were uplifted and highly optimistic after this initial meeting; the designer seemed genuinely interested in meeting our needs. When the initial plans arrived, we were surprised to discover what we outlined in the meeting was minimally present in the plans. When we spoke to the designer about this, we were told to simply use them as a starting point, provide our feedback, and then modifications would be made to best address our needs. So we did.

When the second round of plans arrived, we were dumbstruck. In spite of our direct feedback, these plans incorporated none of it…at all. We felt frustrated and disappointed. In a thoughtful and carefully crafted email, we expressed our unhappiness with these revised plans, and how our expressed needs were not being taken into consideration. Succinctly put, we felt as if we were not being listened to. And how the designer responded to this email only reinforced our experience.

She wrote back, "Sorry to hear of your frustration. We work hard to ensure our clients are satisfied with the work done. We have put thoughtful work into this project. We would be happy to explain to you the reason and rationale behind our efforts, so you can better understand why we did what we did. We have some time later this week." In other words, she was asking us to understand them better, not to understand us better. Whoa! Wait a minute! What's going on here? Not once did the designer express any desire in writing to understand why we were feeling frustrated. Not once did this person express any desire to want to know more about how we felt our needs weren't being taken into consideration. Instead we simply received an offer to hear them out, to better understand them. Huh?

Let's take into account this contractor is well respected, had ample glowing references, and clearly had great confidence in the work that they did. They probably aren't accustomed to receiving negative feedback from their clients. As often happens in situations like this, the expert will exert their credentials and expertise as a way to bring about understanding. This may be fine for brain surgery, but can backfire elsewhere. And in this case, after multiple interactions where we felt our feedback wasn't taken into account, it did. We ceased our working relationship with this designer and sought assistance elsewhere. Had they only inquired as to why we were frustrated, and taken the time to really listen to what we were saying, we may have continued the relationship. But they didn't. Instead, they asked us to understand them, not the other way around. More often than not, this will undermine their credibility and prematurely end what could have been a positive working relationship.

Ethos

Consider the people you trust and find credible. Now compare them to people you distrust or find deceptive. The difference between the two groups is huge, is it not? So, gaining another person's trust and being seen as credible in their eyes should be of paramount importance. It is, in fact, essential. And when we are talking about our communication practices, it is important to recognize what specifically about our communication builds trust and establishes credibility. To that point, and this is crucial to remember, no relationship, business, personal or otherwise, will remain intact if trust and credibility are absent.

And here's another important point: you are only as credible and trustworthy as other people perceive you to be credible and trustworthy. It does not matter how you think of yourself, but what others think of you that matters. The elements that will help elevate or diminish your credibility and trust is as much a matter of *how* you communicate as it is *what* you communicate. Actions do speak louder than words, and more often than not the *how* will outweigh the *what* of your message. Your tone, your speech rate, the words you choose, and the medium through which you communicate will greatly

> *Actions do speak louder than words, and more often than not the* **how** *will outweigh the* **what** *of your message.*

influence the level of credibility and trust others have in you. For better or for worse, credibility also comes from your appearance, from your education and experience, and from what clients, customers, and colleagues say about you. Credibility also comes from your online presence such as LinkedIn profiles, websites, and social media accounts.

Trust is a bit more slippery to establish. I firmly believe we earn it by making others understand we think they are important to us. One way to do this is to demonstrate that we are committed to really listening to them and understanding what they want and need, that we are focused on them and not on ourselves. Another way we build trust is to show we value people.

Let me tell you a quick story about David L. Cohen, Senior Executive Vice President of Philadelphia-based Comcast Corporation. Cohen is a very busy person, to say the least, but I had the opportunity to meet David at a local business function where he was speaking. During our brief conversation we exchanged business cards. The following day, I sent a short email to David, thanking him for his presentation, and the commitment Comcast has made to the City of Philadelphia. I didn't really expect a reply, but I was hoping he might remember me. Within the day, David replied back. This is a man who is #2 at Comcast, one of the largest and most powerful companies in the United States. A man who has sat down before more Senators, members of Congress, and Presidents than most of us combined ever will. And who was I? Compared to Comcast, I was smaller than small. Yet, he replied. Whether it was

David, or his executive assistant, typing the message really doesn't matter. I received a reply! Cohen is clearly committed to making everyone he meets feel valued, and that boosts his credibility. And when you look at his success, you can see that it works! We'll talk about *ethos* more in Chapter 4.

Pathos

You know that saying, the one that goes, "People may not remember your name, the company you worked for, or even where they met you, but they will remember how you made them feel." Well, in some ways that is *pathos*. *Pathos*, simply put, is eliciting a desired emotional state in another person. When Aristotle wrote about *pathos*, he was tapping into a key element of persuasion, that the emotional state of others significantly impacts their ability and willingness to listen to us. In other words, if we overlook how our communication alters another person's emotional state, we quite

> *...the emotional state of others significantly impacts their ability and willingness to listen to us.*

possibly are negating our entire communication effort. Think about it. When we are in a good mood, we are probably more willing to listen to information we don't necessarily agree with as compared to when we are in a bad mood. Or, as Aristotle is quoted in Lane Cooper's seminal 1932 book *The Rhetoric of Aristotle*, "…we give very different decisions under the sway or pain or joy, and liking or hatred."

Once again, and it can't be said enough, *pathos* is about other people's emotions. The emotions we express certainly count, but most important are the emotions we unleash in others, and that is often not in our control. And to truly understand the impact of that, it demands us to employ empathy. Empathy is one part the ability to understand (and I might add, to respect) what other people are feeling. More importantly, empathy is the ability to put ourselves in another person's emotional shoes to feel what the other person is feeling. Too often, we forget the immense power emotions have on people, and the power our communication has to impact the moods of others. A simple smile or hello can go a long way towards building good relationships. A short quip via email, or an unreturned phone call can have the unintended consequence of eliciting a negative emotional reaction, whose origin will be directly traced back to us, and may ultimately erode our credibility and/or limit their receptivity to our message. More often than not, we don't want that, but rather the opposite.

One of the people who really impressed me with

his empathy was "Joe the Squirrel Guy." My wife and I didn't realize just how much noise squirrels make when they get into your house, until we had some in the ceiling above our bedroom. As the exhausted parents of two young children, we believed we could sleep through anything that was not one of our kids crying (or the fire alarm) until we were both utterly exhausted but wide awake at 2:00 am, staring at the ceiling and listening to the two most athletic small furry animals since Chip and Dale having a raucous nut-stashing party above our heads. It took us a little while to find the right person, and it took a little while for Joe to come because Philadelphia is apparently full of squirrels who love throwing raucous nut-stashing parties in people's houses. So we had some more exhausting sleepless nights. Then Joe came, did his work, and *voilà*– blissful silence at night, minus the kids.

Three weeks later, the squirrels were back and we were back to staring at the ceiling, exhausted but wide awake, at 2:00 am. I called Joe the following morning and I was trying hard not to be "that guy," but he could tell I was plain worn out. "I know how hard it is with young kids," he said and he came back to our house that day. Joe found the new hole the squirrels had chewed through in our thick wood cornice. Apparently squirrels will chew through anything that isn't heavy-gauge steel to get at the nuts they stashed. Joe fixed the hole, didn't charge us a penny more, and we haven't had a problem since. Joe was clearly committed to doing a good job and he did. What I remember more, however, is how Joe understood and respected what my wife and I were feeling and experiencing. We'll talk about *pathos* more in Chapter 5.

Logos

Roughly speaking, *logos* refers to the use of reason or logic. Reason and rationality are what distinguish us from all the other species on our planet. Our beautiful cerebral cortex is what gives us the ability to make logical arguments as a means to persuade others or get others to see our point of view. It is a truly powerful tool we use every day, often without giving it a second thought. And what's so intriguing about *logos* is that what may seem logical and reasonable under one set of circumstances may not be so in another, and vice-versa.

Aristotle spoke to the power of *logos* when suggesting that the logic or reason presented does not necessarily need to be true, but only true to those who are receiving it, or more importantly, how they perceive it. And again, it's not always in our control. In fact, there are many instances when improper logic is viewed as both reasonable and rational when it is not. That is to say, under the right conditions, a completely illogical

position, or what are academically referred to as fallacies, can appear logical, so long as *ethos* and *pathos* are
in their proper place. Also, bear in mind, what may
seem reasonable and rational to us may not be so for

other people. Therefore, it
is always important to ask
ourselves the questions,
"Does this seem reason-
able to them?" when em-
barking on the *logos* track.

> *...what may seem
> reasonable and
> rational to us may not
> be so for other people.*

Is the information we are presenting clear, accurate,
and relevant to others? Does it contain the information
they need and want to know? This is not necessarily the
same as telling them everything there is to know about
the topic.

A good example of applied *logos* took place during
a family trip to San Francisco, when I took my then 3
year-old son, Asa, to ride the BART train. San Francisco
was Asa's place of birth and my home for 20 years, and
when we moved to Philadelphia he was far too young
to remember ever riding BART. Given he was now
a full-fledged public transit enthusiast, I had to take
him on a ride. When we got to the ticket machine, a
man claiming he had a $10 BART ticket that he would
sell to us for only $3 approached us. Being a veteran
city dweller, I've seen this play before, so I told him
we were only buying a $2 ticket and that his proposi-

tion wouldn't work for us. Applying additional logic, he persisted, saying for an extra $1 we could have $10 worth of rides. Again, I told him we only needed a $2 ticket. He continued to tell us how for an extra $1 we would have $7 additional dollars in rides. He then put the ticket into the vending machine to verify there was indeed $10 on it, and continued to tell me what a great deal this was. He looked at Asa and mentioned how many more rides my son would be able to take now that his daddy had an additional $7 in fare. It was true, Asa loved riding BART (he calls it the "speedy train"), and Asa and I would actually need to ride BART a couple more times. I relented, handed the man $3, and as if to reinforce his sincere logic, walked us right to the fare gate and made sure the ticket actually worked, and indeed it did. *Ethos*, the first proof, may not have been initially present, and *pathos*, the second proof, was not exactly working for him, but his *logos*, the third proof, was quite clear and ultimately overshadowed the other two. We'll talk about *logos* more in Chapter 6.

Communication competence and Aristotle's three elements walk hand in hand. Some people have a high demand for *ethos* from people. These men and women are the people in business who say, "Prove to me you are credible and earn my trust. Then don't bother me with the details. Just go do the job!" On the other hand, some people want to know every detail of everything every step along the way. They are *logos* heavy. It is not that we haven't earned the trust of people like this; it is just that they want to know all the information as well. From the following examples, we can begin to see what our preferred or default communication styles are: How do we like to communicate? Do we like to be direct and get to the point? Or do we like to get to know a person before we talk about brass tacks? Do we want just the key points or the whole picture? Are we impressed by a highly confident person or does too much confidence make us suspicious? How much confidence do we express when we talk?

We instinctively respond to someone who has the same communication style we do. Most of us don't do it consciously, we just know we "like" the person and say, "they speak my language." We also feel, almost instantaneously, when a person has a vastly different style and that can have the opposite effect. Give a person who just wants the key points a 30-minute presentation and you will bore and frustrate the hell out of her. Give a detail guy just the highlights and he will huff "You didn't answer my questions." A person who loves empathy will be hurt and offended if you look at him and say, "Yeah, I can fix that. Just give me a minute." And a person who just wants you to fix a problem does not want to spend ten minutes listening to a story about how one time you had the exact same problem, and oh how difficult it was.

None of these communication styles is right or wrong. They are just our personal styles– our exceptionally human styles. You can see from these examples why exceptionally human communicators adapt their communication styles to those they are communicating with. Adapting our communication style to the style of another person isn't about manipulating them. It isn't about lying to them. It isn't about tricking or fooling them. We aren't playing mind games. And we aren't selling ourselves out in any way. What we are doing is simply making the wants and needs of the other person in the interaction more important than our own. We are showing we understand them and value them enough to make that effort. When we do, we increase the likelihood they will feel positive about the interaction and that the interaction will be a successful one. What we are doing is being a competent communicator through the application of Aristotle's three elements. What we are being is *exceptionally human!*

Chapter 4

How Credible Can You Be

"All credibility, all good conscience, all evidence of truth come only from the senses."
–Friedrich Nietzsche

What is credibility and how do we build it? Aristotle said that credibility can come from the manner and style in which we present ourselves. If we act credible and trustworthy, it increases the chances that we will be perceived as credible and trustworthy. Aristotle also stressed the importance of "probity" which means we have strong moral principles, honesty, and decency. Today, we would probably use a word like integrity to describe these qualities. If we are seen as having integrity, our credibility rises. On the other hand, if we are seen as lacking integrity, our credibility falls, provided it doesn't crash completely.

In today's world, integrity extends to how quickly we reply to other people and how much we focus on their needs compared to our own. Our actions, as well as our words, build our credibility. Our credibility is also impacted by how people perceive we feel about them – which may or may not be how we meant them to feel, or even about how we actually feel about them.

In this chapter we'll explore ways we can increase our credibility and build trust in the process. It is essential to keep in mind that if we don't earn credibility and build trust in the hearts and minds of the people we meet, the chances are good that anything we say to them will fall on deaf ears. We will focus on two areas of credibility. The first is response time. The second is focus.

If You Care You Will Answer RIGHT NOW

One measure that distinguishes world-class athletes from the weekend warrior is a highly developed response reflex. Professional athletes will respond to events and circumstances around them in impressively short time-periods; whether hitting a ball or stopping a puck, those fractions of a second can be the difference between victory and defeat. The same principle can be applied to our communication with others. More specifically, it can be applied to our digital correspondence with others. It is easy for those of us who grew up before the Internet era to be puzzled by the fact people expect an immediate reply today. However, the right now expectation is real, and has real implications.

Chances are, you receive anywhere between 50 - 100 emails a day, be it work, personal, or otherwise. And chances are you also have your own criteria for determining which email should be replied to first, which later, and which can be disregarded. Recently, I attended a presentation that focused on sales techniques in the digital age. In this program, the presenter laid out a statistic that took me aback. Once a potential client has sent an email request for information, if that email is not replied to within 2 hours, the chances of closing that deal will diminish by 50%. The expectation for a response is so great, that even a 3-hour delay can undermine credibility, and that's before the relationship has even had the opportunity to develop.

When you send a work-related email to someone, how quickly do you expect a reply? And if you don't receive a reply as quickly as you expect, or desire, how do you start to feel about the other person? What happens to their credibility, their trust, and their reliability? My guess is that it takes a little ding, or experiences a slight diminishment. Contrast that with what happens when you receive a reply within the time period you expect. What then happens to their credibility, their trust, and their reliability? It's probably safe to say it goes up, or at the very least, remains where it was prior to you receiving the reply.

So, what are the criteria you use to determine how quickly you reply to an email? Is it the content, or the subject matter? Is it the person who wrote it, be it a superior or subordinate, or a client? Or, is it how important you determine the email to be? My guess is that it's all of the above, if not some combination. But how quickly they want a reply is a good place to start. If you begin by first and foremost thinking about the other person, then it's much more likely that you'll respond within their expected time frame, because after all you are thinking about them first. And in doing so, you both consciously and unconsciously send that person a message that their expectations truly matter, and that will naturally increase our credibility in their eyes. The name of the game here is to build credibility and trust, and having them perceive that their needs matter, you do just that.

When you promptly respond to others, they will be more likely to support and respond to you the next time you need their assistance or input. Consider being a bit more responsive to people over email, even if it is just a brief note letting them know you have read their communication, you will find your relationships to be more positive and effective because those around you feel that they are a priority.

Even more important than a quick response to building credibility: focus on the other person first. If we put the wants and needs of the person first, then the chances of creating an exceptionally positive outcome increase. There are four ways to do this

> *...you will find your relationships to be more positive and effective because those around you feel that they are a priority.*

I'd like to discuss: make the other person feel important, recognize stress, try to see the balance between "understanding" and "solutions" the person wants, and use the word "you" instead of the word "I."

Feeling Important

Most people like to feel important. Some people expect it. Sometimes it is earned, other times it's not. Some people may have a burning desire to feel important, yet they will not, or cannot, express their desire. In our communication with others, we may communicate in a manner that might allow the other person to feel they are important, and at other times we might communicate in a way that might cause the other person to feel they are not important. What's tricky here is knowing first, if the other person wants to feel important, and second, if our communication is indeed expressing that sense of importance. In many ways it comes down to focus. When we place our focus on another person, we are saying to them that they are important, that what they have to say is important, and that what they are feeling is important.

In some cases, it's quite clear who wants to feel important. People who have high status and rank can be amongst those. A title or credential can help tell us if someone is important. At the same time, I don't know too many people who like to feel unimportant. As a matter of fact, when we communicate in a manner that tells the other person they are important, and they don't necessarily expect that, our credibility will go that much higher as a result. We are defying their expectation, in a positive way. When we make everyone feel important, we build credibility across the board, regardless of status, power or position. So, consider making everyone feel important, not just those who we believe to be important. We never know when we will need to work collaboratively with others in the future, and making everyone feel important builds credibility and trust.

How do you help people feel important? Make sure the conversation is focused on them, and reply in a timely manner. Doing these two simple things will go a long way to boost your credibility in their eyes. It doesn't take much to make people feel important.

Consider this story: I was having lunch at my favorite Korean restaurant and business was bustling. Every seat

> *It doesn't take much to make people feel important.*

was taken and folks were standing around both waiting to order and waiting for their orders. From my counter seat, I watched the cooks cranking food out, all 8 burners sizzling up various dishes: Bibimbap, spicy pork, and Korean tacos. The owner was scrambling, putting piping hot dishes on the service trays, along with a side of Kimchee and either marinated beans, or cold marinated cucumber. He then called out order numbers so customers could claim their prize. It was a smooth operation.

After the owner called out number 74, a customer walked up, retrieved her food, and just before walking away, paused. She glanced down and up and down again. The owner turned away to prepare another tray when the customer inquired, "Can I have the cucumbers instead?" Her tray had the beans, not the cucumbers. The owner turned back to her, and then looked down at the cucumber container that lay empty on the counter. He then started to say, "Sorry, we're out of…" then stopped. He then momentarily ducked behind the counter, emerging with a small to-go container with cucumber in it. He took out a small dish, emptied the cucumbers onto it, and handed it to his customer. It all took less than 10 seconds. She was happy.

Less than 10 seconds. The owner could have easily completed his sentence, "Sorry, we're out of cucumbers," and moved on. It probably would have not been a big deal. It would certainly be understandable, given how busy it was, as items run out. I'm sure she would have understood and thought nothing of it. But that's not what happened. He made a split second decision that then took less than 10 seconds to execute, and for that, she did think something of it. She said thank you, he smiled, and I think it's safe to say the reason his restaurant is so busy is because of decisions like that… decisions that take less than 10 seconds to execute, but are certainly noticed.

See Stress in Other People – Help Them Reduce It

We live in a stressful world. We all experience stress. None of us enjoy it. And many of us do not think or act our best when we are under stress. Stress causes us to enter into a fight or flight response. When we are under stress we increase our efforts or we withdraw from a situation. At work, this can translate into trying to work harder and harder, perhaps even becoming somewhat of a "bull in a china shop" character. Or we might retreat into our own inner world and shut others out. I know that when I'm under stress, I tend to fall into the "fight" category and my actions and behavior can come across as aggressive, terse, and blunt. Very rarely will I actually tell people that I'm under stress. Who likes to admit it?

An exceptionally human part of stress is that it affects how we behave in situations, regardless of whether those situations are a cause of the stress or not. For example, before a big presentation with a potential client, I can be very keyed up. I'm feeling the positive stress that– at the right level– gives me energy and focus. But in this state, for example, there have been times I have wanted to yell "come on, let's go" when the line at the coffee shop feels like it is moving slowly. The person serving the coffee isn't causing my stress. My stress has nothing to do with him. But if he smiles and says "Sorry for the wait" then his credibility rises with me. I walk away feeling good about him, better about myself, and more satisfied with our very simple exchange.

So try to be extra responsive to people when they look stressed out or are acting as if they are having a bad day. When we block them out, we allow them to create their own story about our lack of response, which can lead

> *...try to be extra responsive to people when they look stressed out or are ... having a bad day.*

to all kinds of misperceptions and misunderstandings. When we let them in, exceptionally positive interactions arise from even the smallest moments.

Is The Person Seeking Understanding? Solutions? Or Both?

It's probably fair to say that problem-solving conversations are a common communication practice for us all. When you are engaged in conversations, a good question to ask ourselves is what does the other person want from the conversation? In a stereotypical example, one which I personally don't find accurate, it is often stated that when women discuss problems they are looking for understanding, not solutions, and that when men talk about problems, they are looking for solutions not understanding. Well, take all that gender stereotyping and throw it out the window, as it can only lead to trouble; I know plenty of women who want solutions and plenty of men who want understanding. The more important point, though, is that in problem-solving conversations people will want understanding, solutions, or some combination of the two. The trick here is how to figure out which one is desired, for if we can do that, our credibility goes up.

One thing you could potentially do is ask directly if the other person wants a solution or if they simply want to be listened to for the sake of being listened to. That could work, however, there are times when a person won't know which one they want, and the asking of that question could possibly lead to some frustration towards us, and diminish our credibility. Another tack, and I would argue a safer one, would be to begin with aiming for understanding, as I think that if someone really wanted understanding and you started by providing solutions, the immediate pull-back would be harder to reign in than if you did the opposite. Going directly for solutions could cause the person to begin feeling as though what they are experiencing doesn't matter, and once you start to go down that road, regaining trust can be difficult. If someone wants solutions and you provide understanding, they may initially be a bit frustrated, but their feelings won't necessarily be hurt. And they would probably then ask you for a solution with little to no damage to the relationship.

Staying in the moment shows true, focused attention on the other person and your credibility rises in their eyes. You are in essence saying to them, "You matter to me." Consider staying more focused on the present moment and less on how to solve the problems. Although solutions may seem readily apparent, best to err on the side of caution and fully investigate the problem to assure what solutions are actually needed.

Are We Focused on Ourselves, or on Other People?

Here's an exercise for you. The next time you have a conversation with someone, afterwards, ask yourself if you have shared more about yourself or have you discovered more about the other person. My guess is that there is a strong probability that you won't be able to accurately answer this question, as it's not something we often think about.

However, in learning to answer this question, we can tap into something quite powerful. Because in this day and age of iThis and iThat, of customization, options, and personalization, we are probably more self-concerned than ever, and probably feel even more justified than ever in being so. We love ourselves, and there's absolutely nothing wrong with that. Problems begin when we forget that there are other people too, and that other people love to be loved as well. This is not to say that we start loving everybody, but rather that if we can begin to shift our focus slightly more on other people, the results can be quite positively surprising.

Have you ever had a situation in which you are sharing something that recently happened to you, and the other person replies, "Oh, I've had the same thing happen to me," or "Oh yeah, let me tell you about a time when something similar occurred with me." This is called stage-hogging, and not only is it considered an ineffective listening practice, it can also be quite damaging. And what's tricky about this, is that everyone does it. And you don't do it because you are so self-absorbed you cannot get beyond yourself, but you do it because you believe it's a way of connecting or creating common ground with the person you are listening to. But what is actually happening is you are placing your experience before theirs, and this can be quite agitating to the other person, and in their agitation with you, your credibility is diminished.

You gain credibility by prioritizing others and putting aside your own need to share or tell about yourself. Prioritizing others makes them feel that you value them, and they are important and interesting. You are seen as a person to trust and talk to. That means you need to be extra-conscious about what you say. Are your words self-focused or other-focused? Are you sharing more about yourself, and as a result, discovering less about them, or are you placing yourself aside just enough so other people have the necessary space to share about themselves? Ask specific questions about them, or if discussing a particular subject, issue, or topic, request their input or feedback. The goal here is to get others to know that you truly desire to know more about them.

The Word "I" Versus The Word "You"

Another effective way to increase your credibility has to do with your pronoun usage in written correspondence such as email. To this end, I want you to consider how often you use the pronoun "I" in your communication compared to the pronoun "you."

Are you aware of the ratio of "I" usage versus "you" usage? In other words, do you generally or strategically use one pronoun more than the other? I'm bringing this up because research conducted by Dr. James Pennebaker at the University of Texas at Austin uncovered some intriguing findings regarding pronoun usage. In his work, Dr. Pennebaker found the people who use the pronoun "I" more often in written correspondence are perceived to be more self-centered and self-absorbed than if they had used the pronoun "you" or no pronouns at all. For example, if a colleague sends you an email asking about a particular work-related challenge they are experiencing, and you reply, "I think that what I would do in the situation…," you are sending the message that you are overly self-focused and that you filter everything through yourself. Now, this is not a judgment, but rather an insight into the power of pronoun usage. If you were to instead reply, "This situation seems difficult for you. Are you asking for advice, support, or suggestions as to what you can do?", the focus remains solidly on the other person. (Interestingly enough, Pennebaker's research also uncovered that people who use the pronoun "I" less frequently often are in higher status positions, whereas people who use the pronoun "I" with frequency are in lower status positions.)

Most important to recognize, when we overuse the pronoun, "I," especially in email communication because there is an enormous interpretative gap, we can come off as sounding more self-interested/involved, and therefore lose some credibility. Keep in mind that for most of us, our favorite word is our own first name and that our favorite subject is often ourselves. As a result, consider using the pronoun "you" when possible, as it shifts the focus away from self and on to others. By using the pronoun "you" more than "I" in written and oral communication, we keep the focus on the other person, helping that person feel more valued. In doing so, we once again create an opportunity to increase our credibility. *Ethos* is the foundation for all truly effective communication exchanges. By applying the techniques described in this chapter, we will begin to

> *By using the pronoun "you" more than "I" in ... communication, we keep the focus on the other person, helping that person feel more valued.*

strengthen our credibility in other people's eyes, and open the door to deepening trust as well. And once we have our credibility house in order, we become that much more exceptionally human. Now we can begin to focus on what is perhaps one of the most slippery aspects of the human condition, and those are emotions, or *pathos*.

Chapter 5

Emotions *Are* The Message

"Without access to our emotions, our rational processes are handicapped, and we become little better than a conglomeration of arbitrary and random behaviors."
—Julie Schwartz Gottman and John Gottman

Emotions are powerful. In communication, the most powerful emotions are the ones we generate in other people. These emotions affect how we are perceived, how our messages are received, and even how people respond to us before we say a word. As Michelle Garcia Winner and Pamela Crooke astutely point out in their book, *Social Thinking at Work*, "Attempting to interpret each other's emotions is as much a part of the workday as doing our actual jobs."

We've all had interactions with people that have left us feeling worse than we did before. When we have these interactions, they can have a significant impact on our well-being and how we perceive the world and other people. When we experience positive emotions, our ability to tolerate life's unpredictable moments is far greater than when we experience negative emotions. When our emotional experience can be pinpointed to a particular person or event, it creates a lasting impact. How the person or event is perceived, for better or worse, can result in prolonged negative associations that take tremendous time, energy, and effort to undo. Sometimes these negative associations are merely annoying. Sometimes they are catastrophic.

To Dispute or Not to Dispute

Here is an example in which the impact of negative emotions was significant. A friend, who has a professional services company, entered into a contractual agreement with a client preparing for a large, important event. The agreement was standard and straightforward with a clearly worded termination clause complete with deadline. As the preparations unfolded, the termination deadline passed without a notice from the client.

The service delivery date was fast approaching, and it appeared to my friend that the stress of the event was taking a toll on the client. Three weeks prior to the event, my friend received a simple two sentence email from the client asking if they could speak the next day. When they spoke, the client informed her that her services were no longer necessary. When my friend reminded the client that the company had a signed agreement with a clear termination date, which had already passed, the client told her they were prepared to offer her 4% of the contract value in exchange for her time invested thus far. As you might imagine, my friend was not pleased, but the client told her that's all they could do.

My friend got off the phone quite upset. She had blocked time out, coordinated with other contractors, and was hours and hours into the preparation process. Not only that, this was a rather large contract that significantly impacted her business's revenue projections. When she got home, she had trouble playing with her children, eating dinner, and sleeping that night. This emotional state stretched into the following days. And although she was assured by her lawyer that the contract terms would hold up and entitle her to fair compensation, she was upset by how the situation was handled. Over the next few weeks, when anyone mentioned that client's name, or she read about him or her, a deeply negative emotional response followed.

The contract dispute was eventually resolved and in the process my friend discovered the client had very legitimate reasons for not following through. However, the client failed to share this with her until the damage had already been done. From a purely financial standpoint, the client wound up paying my friend a larger portion of the contract value than she might have demanded if she had been treated well from the beginning. The client also damaged the relationship with my friend, which left her less willing to consider future opportunities. And the negative emotions generated significantly decreased my friend's ability to empathize with her client, which ironically is what the client ultimately wanted, but didn't exactly know how to ask for.

Why Are Emotions So Powerful?

We all agree that emotions are powerful and have powerful effects on our interactions with other people. A fascinating question is *why* are they powerful? To answer that question, the pioneer work of the psychologist Albert Ellis is worth exploring.

Ellis was the creator of Rational Emotive Behavioral Therapy. What Ellis discovered is the world of our experiences is composed of three things: facts, interpretations, and emotions. *Facts* are those things are can be objectively agreed upon. For instance, a *fact* would be that when the northern hemisphere is tilted away from the sun, we are in the season called winter. *Interpretations* are the judgments or meanings we give to certain facts. In the case of winter, one could deem winter to be pleasant or undesirable. *Emotions* are how we feel about the facts. And, because facts are interpreted, how we feel about something is utterly dependent on how we interpret it. So if we interpret winter to be enjoyable, then the emotions we experience regarding winter are positive ones. On the other hand, if we interpret winter to be negative, then our emotions will be negative. Coming from someone who spent practically his entire life on the west coast, you might guess how I initially felt about east coast winters.

Now, the key to Ellis' work is how much time our minds spend in the world of fact versus the world of interpretation. How much time do you believe you spend in the world of facts versus interpretation? Is it 50-50? Might you spend 30% of your time in the world of facts and 70% in interpretation? Is it the reverse? What Ellis discovered is that we spend about 90% of our time in the world of interpretations and only 10% in the world of facts. Loosely speaking, 90% of the time we are the greatest Hollywood scriptwriters on earth, and the script we are writing is the story of our life. And however we write

> *...we spend about 90% of our time in the world of interpretations and only 10% in the world of facts.*

that story dictates the emotions we experience. And the

67

same goes for everyone else, reinforcing the fact how little control we have over other's perceptions, and how important it is to know where we do have some control and exercise it.

Emotions color everything. Emotions color how we think and what we see. Emotions allow us to feel deeply about someone while at the same time blind us to other aspects of that person. While under the influence of strong emotions, our perceptions become tainted, and our ability to see a clear picture becomes tainted as well. We can all recall the power of falling in love, and how when we are under those fabulous emotions, our behaviors can become less than rational (what's another sick day?). The same goes when we are experiencing the power of anger or resentment, our rationality becomes suspect.

Simply put, the power of emotions to affect how people respond to our messages is enormous – both positively and negatively. Exceptionally human communicators can create the desired emotions in others.

The Emotions We Expect To Feel Influence Us Too

Let's add another wrinkle to this dynamic. Research suggests that the emotions we expect to feel have a strong influence on the emotions we actually feel. For example, if we expect to be disappointed by another person, we will look for information that confirms that expectation, just as when we expect to be satisfied with a person we will look for reasons to be satisfied. It is an idiosyncratic feature of our brilliant minds that we will desire to feel a particular way based upon past experience and then write a "story" for ourselves that justifies feeling the way we want to feel.

This means that the negative feelings people had about us last week or last year influence how they receive our messages today, which is bad news. On the other hand, positive feelings from the past also influence how people receive our messages, which is good news. Perhaps the best news, though, is that unless people have done significant reading about emotions, they probably have precious little insight into why they feel a particular way. They just feel it. This gives us opportunities to use simple techniques that create positive emotional interactions with people that satisfy them and satisfy us. Let's talk about some of these techniques right now.

"I" Versus "You" Again – with a Twist!

We know that the words we choose have big impact on how people hear our messages. In Chapter 4, we talked about how using the pronoun "you" instead of

"I" in our communication with others makes us sound less self-centered and self-absorbed and so increases our credibility.

This is not an absolute rule, however. There are situations in which using the pronoun "you" can actually damage our credibility and cause others to experience negative emotions ranging from defensiveness to anger. In what is known as the *Language of Responsibility*, the use of "you" during disagreements or in situations when things don't go according to plan can lead other people to feel as though you are solely blaming them and not taking responsibility yourself, which then leads to negative emotions.

People tend to feel better when blame is not being directly assigned to them. Our use of the pronoun "I" more than "you" can come across as being self-accountable or taking responsibility, which will lower people's defenses. When we overuse the pronoun, "you" vs. "I," we are perceived as less accountable or responsible, and more of a finger-pointer, increasing the chances others will become more defensive. So we need to be careful that when we use "you" in these situations that we use "I" as well, to create a sense of balance.

Understanding Others Versus Being Understood Ourselves

Another step we can take towards generating positive emotions in people is how we prioritize those people. This brings us back to a key question: what is more important– understanding others or being understood by others?

Think about conversations you've had where there was an underlying misunderstanding. Do you have a tendency to want to make yourself understood first, before understanding the other person's position? If you are like most people, including me, you probably find yourself wanting to be understood first. I think it's safe to say that most people fall into this category. We all want to be understood and will take whatever steps are necessary to make that happen. At the same time, how often have you pressed and pressed to be understood, only to find yourself feeling frustrated because you have not been able to get the other person to see where you are coming from? Not only that, how many times have you been in the position of wanting to be understood only to find the other person is doing nothing more than trying to get you to understand them? And when that occurs, how do you feel? Frustrated? Angry? Disappointed? Probably so, and this significantly impacts how you now perceive the other person, both in terms of how you feel about them but also the credibility you assign them. Recall the interior designer we worked with, their insistence on being understood first,

71

and how they lost us as a client as a result.

And now I'm sure you can see the point. This dynamic works both ways. In those times we are trying to diligently to be understood, we may very well be generating negative emotions in others that will significantly inhibit both their ability and desire to understand us. The point being, in those instances when we want to be exceptionally human communicators, or really anytime, prioritize understanding the other person first, even if that means we ourselves are not being understood right away.

By making sure you understand why a particular issue, subject, or issue is important to another person first, that person will feel listened to, which in turn has them feeling better about you than otherwise might happen. This will increase the possibility that, in turn, they will desire to understand where you stand. Consider working a bit more to understand others before attempting to be understood.

> *Consider working a bit more to understand others before attempting to be understood.*

When you push to have yourself understood, you may have their attention in the short run, but you are asking them to delay expressing themselves, which may cause them to feel less important, and in turn, take what you have to say less seriously. If this sounds familiar, it should. Making other people feel important is one of the key points from the *ethos* chapter!

Consistency Versus Variability in Communication Style

It is often said that being consistent is an admirable trait. Whether the consistency has to do with our character or our communication style, we think being consistent leads to higher credibility. Nobody wants to be viewed as one who waffles or is a flip-flopper, as we so often hear presidential candidates point out in their rivals. As it is for products so it is for people and our relationships with them: consistency is the key to building loyalty and trust. So it makes good sense that we would want to be consistent, as it increases our credibility in the eyes of others. However, there are times when being consistent will actually work against us, and this is especially true in our communications with others.

Each of us has our own preferred communication style. Be it assertive, passive, aggressive, accommodating, or whatever, our style is preferred because it's familiar, we have success with it, and it causes us little discomfort and requires little effort. Simply put, it's something we can do without much thought. Now, there's nothing wrong with this approach whatsoever. And at the same time, just because our preferred style works for us does not mean it will work well for others. Our accommodating style may cause others to feel annoyed, confused, or some other undesirable emotion, and if we are attempting to be an exceptionally human communicator in that moment, we'll fail if we don't adapt our style. It goes back to those characteristics of the competent communicator. The competent communicator has access to an entire range of communication styles and the ability to perform those styles when needed. They are equally able to be assertive and amenable. The key is whatever style you choose should be selected with the intention of generating a desired emotional response in the other person. So to that end, we need to be aware of another person's preferred communication style, and most importantly, how they like to be communicated with.

When you adapt your communication style, people feel more comfortable and relaxed around you, therefore increasing the probability of positively impacting how others feel about you and their receptivity to your message. Having a set or rigid style runs the risk of having people feel less comfortable and relaxed around you, which can increase the probability of nega-

> *When you adapt your communication style, people feel more comfortable and relaxed around you...*

tively impacting how others feel about you and their receptivity to your message. Being more adaptable with your communication style will take effort on your part. First, you need to know what your preferred style is. You also need to note what styles you are uncomfortable with, as those are the styles you want to practice. Take one uncomfortable style and practice it twice a day for 3 weeks. If you are assertive, practice taking a step back, and if you are more inclined to be shy, practice being more assertive. Note how you feel employing that style, what is challenging about it, and what you do to overcome it. After 3 weeks, you'll find this style will begin to feel more comfortable and more accessible to you when you need it.

Focus on the Goal – But at What Cost?

You know how it goes. When a deadline is fast approaching, you begin to feel the stress, as do others who are working with you. So our interactions become more efficient. Gone are salutations and unnecessary words and we cut right to the point. Our reading becomes less effective as well, as we start quickly scanning our emails, looking just for the information that will help meet the goal. And in this process, people might begin to feel slighted, diminished, and minimized, all as a result of how they are being communicated with. And although the goal is reached, the fallout from those negative emotions leads to greater resistance and distance in future interactions. It's human to do this, and not necessarily anyone's fault, but it doesn't need to be that way.

Our first step when we are in stressful situations is to place greater value on the relationship. We are not necessarily placing less value on the goal; we are simply not letting achieving the goal compromise the relationship. Now we are all subject to our curt behavior, outbursts, and sharp exchanges, and those won't necessarily disappear. At the same time, the more effort we place in cultivating our relationships with those we work with, the more valued they begin to feel, and the more positive emotions they actually experience in relation to us. In building up that good will, we not only establish allies along the way, we earn their forgiveness in advance when stress causes us to behave in less than desirable ways.

Even though achieving a goal is ultimately necessary, damaging relationships in the process can be more harmful in the long run. Consider making sure other people know their contributions are valued throughout the process, and you will increase their buy in. Give them positive feedback when it's warranted, or when it's not expected. No need to be Pollyannaish here, just take a few extra minutes to nurture relationships to

keep others feeling posi-
tive about you. When
you prioritize the goal
over the relationship,
you can alienate the very
people you need to work
with you, and in the

> *Consider making sure other people know their contributions are valued throughout the process, and you will increase their buy in.*

process reduce opportunities for future collaboration.
Keeping those emotions as positive as possible is the
key to being exceptionally human.

In Written Communication, Don't Let Emotional Tone Get Lost!

There's a widely pointed to statistic from Dr. Albert
Mehrabian that says over 90% of meaning in a communication exchange is derived outside the words themselves. It's not what you say but how you say it that
matters most. In the recent past, a significantly larger
portion of our workplace communication took place
either face-to-face or over the phone where it was much
easier to communicate emotional tones – especially
positive emotions. Nowadays, face-to-face exchanges
are far less frequent and more often are replaced by
written communication. In texts, social media, instant
messaging, or email, both the sender and the receiver
are at the mercy of the written words.

There's nothing wrong with that, but unlike verbal communication, which has interpretative gaps of its own, written communication's interpretative gaps are Grand Canyons in comparison. That's because the most significant nonverbal quality that impacts how people feel about how we communicate with them is our *emotional tone*. Emotional tone is the overall feel of a message. That feel can be supportive, abrasive, warm, cold, friendly, or challenging, to name a few. In verbal communication, it includes not only the words we choose, but also our volume, rate, pitch, and emphasis (or lack thereof). In verbal communication, people hear our tone and have direct emotional responses as a result.

In written communication, given our real voice is absent, it's our composition style, the words we choose or don't choose, our exclamation points, questions marks, bolding, capitalizing, and grammar. All these allow people to fill in the blank, make interpretations, and then feel whatever it is they are going to feel. And if we are trying to be exceptionally human communicators, the feeling we desire is positive. So, how can we communicate positively? We can place ourselves in their emotional shoes and ask ourselves, "How might the way I'm communicating this cause *them* to feel?" Note how it's not about how we think we would feel, but rather how they might feel. In doing this, we are simultaneously placing our focus on them so they feel valued, while we are also increasing our credibility in their eyes. As I like to say, it's all interrelated.

When you are conscious of your emotional tone in a written message you have taken the recipient's feelings into consideration. The how you say what you say gives you a higher probability of having your message received by others in the way you intended. This is not about being touchy-feely or politically correct, this is about being strategic. Staying conscious helps bring people closer to you, as they will feel more comfortable communicating with you, even when the subject matter is difficult. By placing insufficient attention on your emotional tone, you may be inadvertently pushing people away from you, because they may find the tone of your message off putting. Although this takes additional effort, this practice will allow you to keep people engaged, even if the subject matter is disagreeable. To recognize how this works, consider the tone difference between reading the word "Thanks" versus "Thanks!" They read differently, do they not? They feel different. That's the power of tone.

Keeping these *pathos* techniques in mind allows us to be exceptionally human with our communication and generates desired emotions in others. These techniques include using the word "I" in conversations about responsibility, focusing on understanding other people before being understood ourselves, adapting our communication style to the style of the people we meet, emphasizing both the goal and the relationship when working with people, and finally paying close attention to how people might read the emotional tone of our written communications and work to make sure the tone they read is positive. Practicing these techniques will help ensure your communication is that much more exceptionally human!

Chapter 6

Logically Speaking

"Give me a reason to love you"
—Portishead

"Purpose is often misunderstood...
It's not a goal but a reason."
—L. Hill, G. Brandeau, E. Truelove,
and K. Lineback, Collective Genius

In the two previous chapters, we stressed the importance of establishing our credibility to generate a desired emotional response. It's vitally important that we frame our communication properly so that it can be digested easily. Logic and reason are what allow us to do just that.

Logic and reason ground and contextualize our communication so the other person can derive a meaning that most matches what we desire. And that meaning must be appropriate to the other person. Again, it's not about us; it's about them; or better yet, their perceptions. No matter how reasonable and rational we might find our communication, it must correlate with what the other person finds reasonable, rational, and appropriate, or it simply will not work. If what we convey is seen as inappropriate, we begin to erode the very credibility we worked to establish, and begin to generate emotions that will cause the other person to be less inclined to listen to us.

Nothing is guaranteed. Think about how many times you thought you knew what someone else meant when later on you came to discover the meaning was much different than you had invested in. To err is human, and we err constantly when it comes to our communication, either as the sender or receiver of messages. Don't feel bad about it; simply accept it. By dropping the judgment, you can view these errors as a fact in and of itself, and begin to strategize about how to do something about it. You can apply sound reason and logic so your communications are properly contextualized. As they say in real estate: location, location, location; so it can be said in communication: context, context, context!

Like all the skills required to become exceptionally human communicators, excellence in the skills of *logos* is required. All of us have struggled to write clear, concise, complete, and compelling messages in our lives, from papers in school to reports and proposals at work, to personal letters in our private lives. Some of us have even worked to write books and I can tell you from first-hand experience, it is a struggle.

Like the skills needed to build trust and generate desired emotions, all of us already possess the ability to express facts and reasons yet all of us have the ability to get even better. We just need to focus on six areas. The first is making sure we understand other people's facts and reasons first through the techniques of **active listening**. The second is to grasp the **context** of the communication. The third is making sure everything we write and say is **relevant** to the task at hand. The fourth is to avoid ambiguity by being **clear and specific**. The fifth is to avoid using logical fallacies and use **sound logic**. And the sixth is to provide an appropriate level of **detail**.

Understand People's Facts First Through Active Listening

The first step to expressing compelling facts and reasons is to make sure we clearly understand what people want or need from an interaction. We all know what it is like to get this part of communication wrong. For example, if you think your spouse has asked you to stop by the grocery store on the way home when he or she actually said to come home first and watch the highly-energized children so he or she can find peace doing the grocery shopping, you'll know what I mean. Often times, we believe we listened to the other person, when in fact we have only heard them (this distinction will become clear in Chapter 7). We all have listening challenges, and it is as human as breathing to not listen as well as we can, but there is something we can do about that. In the Appendix, we'll get into details on how to develop your **active listening** skills.

The Context of The Message Is King

Context is the **who**, **what**, **when**, **where**, and **why** of our communications. Context has a powerful influence on the facts and reasons in our messages, and it is powerful in part because it is often invisible. Context tends to be implicit in our messages rather than explicit. Context is about the assumptions we make about the message we are sending – and as we all know, wrong assumptions lead to wrong messages.

There is a classic communications exercise that demonstrates how context, or lack thereof, powerfully influences our assumptions. The exercise features a photo of an elderly woman crying. The initial look at this photo is very close up on the woman's face. When people are asked to describe how this woman is feeling, they more often than not say she is upset, sad, or grieving.

The next shot is taken a bit further away, and we see the same woman crying in front of what looks to be the door of a church. Again, when asked what this woman is feeling, people use similar adjectives. The next photo is a much wider view, and the woman is one of several people in front of a church where a wedding party is departing. This time around, folks say that the woman is happy, crying tears of joy, and nobody thinks she's sad anymore. That is the power of context and what happens when we make assumptions.

Many times, we understand the context of a message so well we do not need to think about it. When a friend texts, "Wanna get a coffee?" we know which coffee shop he means. We know he wants to get the coffee right now. We know he probably only wants to take ten minutes to drink the coffee. We know it is a casual offer we can decline if we are busy at that moment. And our friend knows we know these things. On the other hand, if our boss texts us "Can you meet me at the coffee shop around the corner in ten minutes?" – during the work day – when both of us are in the office – then that's a whole different context and it dictates a different response.

Or think about this example. If we tell someone to jump into a small raft in the middle of the ocean, they will think we are crazy and ignore us. If we tell them to jump into a raft because we say the ship is sinking, they are going to pay more attention to us because they now understand the context of our message. And if we are wearing the uniform of one of the ship's officers (*ethos*/credibility), and we are speaking in a calm and authoritative manner (generating *pathos*/emotions), people will not only listen to us – they will do what we ask them!

So we should take a moment to think about the who, what, when, where, and why of our messages, particularly the important ones, and make sure we understand the context before we proceed. It can make a tremendous difference in the effectiveness of what we say.

Is Our Message Relevant to the Task at Hand?

Often times, we find ourselves in situations when there is a specific task that needs completing. If we are working with others on this task, our communication might vary. In situations like this, some of us like to keep our communication restricted simply to the task at hand, while others will veer off topic as a way to release any pressure and perhaps add a much-needed distraction. Both are reasonable communication approaches.

There are times when I appreciate and enjoy when the communication goes beyond the scope of the task and turns to other, non-related matters. There are times, especially early in a working relationship, when this can prove beneficial, as we are taking time to get to know the other person. Our task in these cases is to build a rapport with a person that is essential to a good working relationship. If the task is to brainstorm new ideas, then veering off topic is precisely the point of the communication and we want to do more of it.

However, if we talk about non-relevant issues too regularly, or if it begins to become a distraction to actually completing the task, then it becomes a liability. When our communication sticks to the task at hand, providing relevant information and appropriate details, our positions come across as more sound, reasonable and logical, which helps to ensure prolonged dialogue. People feel we are respecting their time. Most of all, people will feel that we are putting their needs and interests first by limiting our messages to topics that interest them rather than just ourselves.

To illustrate, I have a friend who just loves to share what is going on not only in my friend's life, but in the lives of all our mutual friends as well. As a matter of fact, whenever I prepare to speak with this friend, I have to make sure I'm allowing enough time, as these conversations are never brief. And although I often en-joy the musing, there are times when what I really want to do is get to the point, without all the unnecessary storytelling. But that never happens, and that's fine, as this is my friend and trust has been built up over years. I simply accept it. In other situations, where trust hasn't been developed, it is a liability.

Now, there are certainly cultural factors that play into this, as some cultures appreciate taking more time to ease into a conversation, and others appreciate getting right to the point. And beyond cultures, there are individual personalities as well. At the same time, if you start straying off topic too much, your communication effectiveness may suffer. For instance, you probably had conversations in which a person says "I had dinner with X last night and she told me the most incredible news" but then tells you first the story of how they planned the dinner, then how much traffic there was on the way to the restaurant, then about changes on the menu at the restaurant while you are sitting there thinking, "Just tell me the news!"

In our professional lives, these conversations are easier to manage. One way to make sure our communication is relevant is to always offer an agenda at the beginning of a communication. This agenda does not have to be formal. You can say to a colleague, "Do you have twenty minutes to talk about Clients A, B and C?" When our colleague says, "yes" we know the conversation is relevant to her and we can go forward. Another simple trick I like to use is when I have three questions for a person, I send them in three short emails rather than one long email. I also clearly label the topic of each in a subject line such as "Important question about budget of Project Alpha." When the colleague opens the email, I know she has decided the topic is relevant to her.

So it is important for us to always be aware the topic of our communication, and to be strategic and thoughtful about how we approach the other person. Straying off topic, although at times not a bad thing, can dilute our logic and message, and limit our ability to keep people actively engaged with us.

Clear and Specific ... Or the Agonies of Ambiguity

Ideally, all our communication would be clear, specific, and make sense to people. I know, easier said than done! By eliminating ambiguity and providing people with a smooth and simple explanation for things, we assure they have the necessary foundation to make sense of our argument. Their willingness to accept what we have to say will increase. They will feel more grounded and at ease in our presence. They will be more willing to accept difficult messages and stay engaged.

Always keep in mind that we, as human beings, are endlessly filling in the blanks as we attempt to make sense of the world around us. Over time, we become predisposed to do so in distinct ways, distinct to our experiences, to our expectations, and to our preferences. As part of our way to avoid uncertainty, we like to ascribe meaning to things, circumstances, and situations as quickly as possible. As a general rule, we like to avoid uncertainty, which is why when someone communicates something that doesn't make sense, we become less engaged, as we don't want to be burdened with uncertainty.

> ...*we like to avoid uncertainty*...

By grounding our communication in meaning, by giving others a clear reason or rationale, we help them avoid the uncomfortable feelings associated with uncertainty, the stress that it can produce, and the impact that has on their wellbeing. When people are feeling anxious, nervous, or unsettled, they will view information through that lens, and that will absolutely taint how they ascribe meaning to that information. Sometimes this may be to a strategic advantage, but this book isn't about that, it's about recognizing these human aspects, so we can best convey information and best connect with others.

If we go back to the work of Albert Ellis, when he states how 90% of the time we are making up stories about 10% facts, you can see how significant specificity is. The fewer facts you provide people, the more inclined they will be to make up stories that fit their perspectives, which may not necessarily be ours. So, what can you do to help assure those stories are told in the way you would like them to be told, or at the very least increase the odds of that actually happening? Simple. Give people clear and specific facts. Most importantly, attend to their point of view, not yours.

One simple technique that helps me be clear and specific is to use numbers in my messages whenever possible. Quantities, measures, prices, times, and dates are all easy candidates for this approach.

Some examples:

Vague: "We are having a lot of people for Thanksgiving and we need a big turkey."
Specific: "We are having 20 people for Thanksgiving and we need a 20 pound turkey."

Vague: "The budget for his project is tight."
Specific: "The budget for this project is $3,500."

Vague: "Come Tuesday at dinner time."
Specific: "Come next Tuesday, January 19 at 6 pm."

Another simple technique is to ask ourselves what the other person already knows about a topic. It's human to assume that people know the facts that we know, or to forget that they don't know these facts yet. For example, I have a friend who asked her husband if he could watch their kids during the game in which her college's football team was playing their biggest rival. She had known for weeks the game was going to be played in the afternoon and didn't stop to ask herself if her husband knew too. Her husband assumed the game was at night and said, "yes." It turns out he had to work in the afternoon and she wound up playing games with the kids instead of watching the game with her friends. She loves her kids and DVR'd the game, so although slightly disappointed, this wasn't a high stakes issue, but it does show how leaving ambiguity in our communication allows people to fill in the blanks their way!

One of the other advantages of being clear and specific is that it helps people be clear and specific with us in return. When we say, "the budget is $3,500," it makes it easy for the other person to say, "we can work with that," or they can explain they "really need $4,000 for this job." When we are specific, we are better communicators and we help make other people better communicators too!

Logical and Persuasive

Clear and specific facts are the foundation on which we build our reasons why people should agree with us and take the actions we propose. Even better, extraordinarily compelling facts make persuasion simple. We are all familiar with this from building "business cases" in our professional lives. Businesses spend their time and money on something new only when they are convinced of the likelihood of a worthwhile return on investment, or when the risk is balanced by a commensurate potential return. People don't invest in things they think are bad ideas; they only invest in good ideas. (Whether the perceived good idea actually turns out to be good is another matter, of course!)

The same is true in our personal lives. If our partner says to us, "Let's go to the Caribbean this February. We hate winter!" We might reply, "I don't know." If she says, "I found this four-star resort. It has tennis and snorkeling for me. Yoga and surfing for you. A pool and water-slide for the kids. And it has a great deal right now." We would be far more inclined to say yes. One technique I use to test the persuasiveness of my arguments is to ask myself this simple question: if I was the other person and this was the proposal I received and for these reasons, would I agree with it? If my answer is "no" then I know I have more work to do.

When I am on the other side of the question, and I'm the person who is on the receiving end of an argument, I am always on the look out for logical fallacies or what we call in casual conversation BS. The world is filled with smooth talkers and likeable sociopaths, (think Bernie Madoff or any other con artist) who uses flawed logic to get ahead by harming us. We don't want to be these kinds of people, and we don't want to use their tricks. Although their methods might work initially, they will certainly backfire on us once exposed.

One common fallacy, or false logic, is the **red herring**. A red herring is when someone begins to provide very reasonable, sound information about a particular subject that in fact, has very little to do with the matter at hand. Recently, I witnessed a classic red herring in action. A union group was protesting outside a local food business. Like most places in America, unions in Philadelphia have taken a significant credibility hit, earned or unearned. However you feel about unions, one thing they are very good at is vigorously stating their position. In this case, they were unhappy that lower paid non-union workers were used in the construction process, and they were handing out fliers stating their grievances. Instead of focusing on the labor issue, these fliers were dedicated to making statements about this restaurant's prior health code violations. If you're like me, you want to eat at establishments that have a clean bill of health, so reading something like that might cause me to pause before eating there. However, the issue was labor and wage related, not food quality, and it weakened their argument.

Some other notable fallacies include the **slippery slope**, which is when someone takes the position that if one particular event happens, it will lead to a cascading effect, either good or bad. The **false dilemma** is when one presents only two possible options, when, in fact, there are several options available. The **hasty generalization** is when we make broad, sweeping statements based upon a significantly small sample of information available.

There are more, but those are the most common. The thing about fallacies is that credibility and feelings can overshadow the most common ones so they go unnoticed. If we go back to Bernie Madoff, he had this amazing perceived credibility. And because people felt opportunities to have him invest their money were rare, they jumped at the opportunity. Incidentally, this is another classic fallacy, that of **scarcity**. And, as we all know, what at first appeared to be too good to be true was in fact just that. But under the right circumstances, it was initially taken as the opposite. Do your best to be mindful to eliminate fallacies in your own logic, and always build arguments that would pass your most stringent standards.

The Right Level of Detail Is ... What?

Often times, a major culprit in ineffective communication is the holding back of details and important information. In our warp-speed age of information transference, we try to make our communication as efficient and succinct as possible. Consider the number of 1-2 sentence email correspondence we have sent and received, not to mention those wonderfully brief Twitter and text exchanges. And although there's nothing inherently wrong with brevity, if we simply remain succinct, we may not be adequately providing the necessary background information and pertinent details needed to assure mutual understanding.

When it comes to providing a solid grounding for others, a safer bet is to err on the side of more, not less. When you share pertinent details, you help to create a more logical and grounded argument, ensuring others understand where you are coming from and where you are going, while minimizing misunderstandings. Consider regularly sharing details. When you fail to let people know where you are coming from or where you are going, your logic can appear less sound, increasing the chances for misunderstandings. Your interactions, in turn, are less effective and productive, and our credibility suffers.

At the same time, this advice requires us to answer two tricky questions: what are the pertinent details in the communication? And especially, what are the details the other person considers pertinent?

Just as exceptionally human communicators adapt their communication style to the style of their receivers, they also need to calibrate the amount of detail they share to the amount of detail the receiver wants. We have all encountered the "big picture" person who tells us "I trust you. Go do it and don't bother me, just deliver the results you promise." We have all also encountered the "detail fiend" who says "I want to see every step along the way that gets us to the results we want." These styles are neither right nor wrong, of course. They are just the styles people want us to adopt when we are communicating with them.

Similarly, too much information can cause confusion and uncertainty just like too little information can cause confusion and uncertainty. An example of this (and anyone who is not a tech lover will appreciate this) is the experience of trying to buy a new television or computer. A friendly, enthusiastic young person greets us in the store and instantly begins to tell us numbers, speeds, acronyms, these-es and those-es and we have no idea what he's saying. These details aren't as pertinent to us, and because we don't understand them, often times we leave the store with nothing more than additional confusion.

When it comes to offering pertinent details, the good news is you can always ask people what they want. You just need to make sure you put the burden of the question on yourself. "Did I explain that clearly? Have I told you everything you want to know?"

In Summary

The mere fact that we are able to communicate with each other is a miracle beyond miracles. Given all those thoughts racing through our minds, the uniqueness of our experiences, and our vast emotional range, being on the same page with anyone is, quite simply, amazing. That's why it's of vast importance that we do everything within our power to ensure our communication provides clarity.

With every communication ask yourself if you are providing appropriate information, useful information, and sufficient information? By making sure your communication provides clarity, you come across as more reasonable and your positions more sound. This ensures others fully understand the situation and are better prepared to engage in productive dialogue.

Logos, our reason and rationality, are of significant importance in this process. Remember though, without generating desired emotions and establishing credibility, our communications go nowhere. Back in ancient Greece, it was the philosopher Plato who championed *logos*. Logic and reason are deeply seeded in the western tradition. The Enlightenment period in 18th century

Europe employed reason to cut through monarchical and religious dogma to spawn personal and social liberation. But in and of itself, logic is not enough. Try reasoning with a 5-year-old as to why they should or should not do something…good luck. Because the 5-year-old is still developing their rational mind (and will do so for the next 15 years or so), emotions rule the day. And as we mature and develop, and as our minds mature and develop, we can deploy reason and logic in highly impactful ways. It's in the conjunction of the 3 elements of logic, emotion, and credibility that allow us to become *exceptionally human communicators!*

Exceptionally Human

Chapter 7

Why Are We Doing This? Making Exceptionally Human Communication Work for Us

"Where does the solution already exist? Where is the future already happening in the organization right now?"
–M. O'Connor & B. Dornfeld,
The Moment You Can't Ignore

As you can now tell, becoming an exceptionally human communicator requires focus and effort. It's the application of age-old wisdom in an amazingly fast-paced twenty-first century world. Now is the time to put everything we've covered together so you can start enjoying the benefits of being an exceptionally human communicator. To that end, we want to recognize the places and times in which we engage in this extraordinarily powerful communication practice either in our personal life, working within organizations, or managing organizations.

Key Organizational Interactions

In our professional lives, the most important communications are what I call **key organizational interactions**, or KOIs. In this chapter, we'll begin by exploring what KOIs are and the criteria for defining them. We'll also explore the latent value within those KOI interactions, value that is waiting to be extracted. To help demonstrate how we can actually pull all this off, I'll explore a real-life organizational situation that shows establishing credibility, generating desired emotions, and applying flawless logic in action.

Do you know which of your interactions at work have the most significant impact on how you are perceived? Do you know the places within your organization that have the most significant impact on how your organization is perceived, both internally and externally?

Key organizational interactions are those interactions that have the deepest impact on how people and organizations are perceived. KOIs can take place both within the organization itself, or beyond the organization's walls. KOIs can be amongst co-workers, superiors and subordinates, or between the organization and the customers and clients they serve. What differentiates KOIs from everyday interactions is KOIs tend to have a much greater and longer-lasting impact on how the organization is per-ceived compared to other

> *Key organizational interactions are those interactions that have the deepest impact on how people and organizations are perceived.*

interactions. An exchange between an employee and their boss can be a mundane interaction. It evolves to a KOI if the boss is unnecessarily demanding or harsh in such a way that causes the employee to begin to feel negatively about the organization. KOIs can be inter-actions between an hourly, front-line employee and a customer, where an exceptionally positive interaction can outweigh dissatisfaction about a deficient product or service. And the KOIs we have with co-workers, supervisors, clients, and customers make a huge differ-ence in our success.

KOIs can be subtle. The difference between being greeted warmly, or being ignored, when we walk into a restaurant is enormous. A supervisor simply acknowl-edging that her team feels frustrated about a project, and validating that frustration, can be the difference be-tween that team feeling motivated and inspired to com-plete the project, or not. In other words, KOIs are the exchanges that will ultimately be remembered. They become the stories people recall and share with others. They tend to have exceptionally human qualities. These are moments of communication competence. As you'll remember, communication competence is when the manner in which we express the message is satisfying to the other person – not necessarily the substance of the message itself.

Any exchange can potentially become a KOI. Here are but a few examples:

- email exchanges
- phone calls
- face-to-face conversations
- public presentations
- superior/subordinate exchanges
- co-worker exchanges
- client/customer exchanges
- social media
- sales efforts
- marketing efforts

Don't overlook them. They appear all the time! Take a few moments now to list some possible KOIs specific to your organization.

Exceptionally Positive KOIs in the "Value Zone"

CEO and author Vineet Nayar coined the term "Value Zone." Nayar focuses on the Value Zone of large retail businesses in his book *Employees First, Customer Second*. His insights are equally compelling and essential whether you are a business-to-consumer, or business-to-business organization, whether you are part of a team, or managing one. The Value Zone is the place where a company's value is built or broken. It is where interactions between an organization's people and their clients and customers determine the true perceived value of that organization. Success in the Value Zone is essential to people and organizations who want to thrive in a world where the internet, robust e-commerce, automated manufacturing, sophisticated analytical algorithms, and globalization are all powerful competition. Exceptionally human communication in positive KOIs builds the Value Zone. KOIs and exceptionally human communication cannot be outsourced or performed by computers. And more, within the Value Zone the potential for fantastic amounts of new value to be created exists, if we can just see the opportunities!

Nayar stresses the importance of, you guessed it, an organization putting its employees first and its customers second. Customers are still a high priority, of course. However it is the employees who deliver the ultimate value of the services and products that an organization provides. Quite often these people are frontline employees who earn an hourly wage and experience no direct financial benefit beyond that hourly pay. Some organizations intimately know the value of this Value Zone. Companies such as Whole Foods and Zappos come to mind, where seemingly each and every interaction with their frontline employee is one that is pleasant and leaves one feeling truly valued. The point here is that an organization's success or failure is often dependent on how well the least paid employees communicate. So it is not just external exchanges, it is internal ones as well, and these companies are known to treat their employees with as much value as they do their customers. Some companies seem to forget how important their frontline interactions are, and how important their employees are, and I'm sure you have a few in mind.

> *...an organization's success or failure is often dependent on how well the least paid employees communicate.*

There are multiple forms of value that can be extracted via exceptionally human communication. Here are just a few possible forms value can take:

- time
- motivation
- engagement
- trust
- innovation
- energy
- buy-In
- advocacy
- company repute
- brand perception
- sales
- physical health
- revenue
- employee empowerment
- productivity
- goal attainment
- rekindled interest, loyalty
- effort
- creativity

I'm certain there are other forms of value you can identify. Consider what a 5% improvement in any one of these areas would look like for you and your organization. It's not unlike having a 5% return on a financial investment; its sound, reasonable, keeps you ahead of inflation, and has little downside. In an 8-hour or 480 minute workday, 5% equals 24 minutes. How would 24 additional minutes of trust impact how your organization performs? What about 24 additional minutes of innovation, motivation, or creativity? Or what about 24 additional minutes of "Thanks!" versus "Thanks." No doubt, the effort would benefit you and your organization, and it's far more realistic to achieve 5% than 480 minutes worth. And really, communication is the key to unlocking the 5%, and then 5% more, and 5% more. Again, take a few moments now to consider some places you can form additional value.

How Do We Measure the Results of Key Organizational Interactions?

Just how do we measure the impact of exceptionally human communications? Human interactions are nebulous affairs. In one sense, there is no rigorously objective way to measure the impact of being an exceptionally human communicator, for how do you stop or go back in time to find out? At the same time, we know the powerful downside of ineffective communication is very real. We've all experienced the negativity that arises when confronted with ineffective communication practices. And we know there are real costs associated with not communicating effectively. As we talked about a moment ago, envision what a 5% improvement in communication would look and feel like compared to those times when ineffective communication rules the exchange.

This is where we need to take a slight leap of faith and develop our own personal measurements. Do we notice improved workplace relationships, less frustration, greater camaraderie, or increased happiness? You set the bar for yourself. Feel free to make adjustments anywhere along the way. The most important thing is to remain conscious, to seek out opportunities to be exceptionally human, and observe the results.

I would like to give you an example from my own professional experience, one that I think will help make these nebulous measurements less vague. This is about an organization we worked with who recognized their Value Zone and knew measuring results would be challenging. Nonetheless, they knew better communication strategies would have a significant impact on their people and customers.

A Case Study of Exceptionally Human Communications in The Value Zone

Annually, over 31 million travelers pass through Philadelphia International Airport. In September 2015, the airport was expecting a significant bump up in use, as the Catholic Church's once-every-three-years World Meeting of Families was coming to Philadelphia, and with it a visit by the widely popular Pope Francis.

The Airport's Executive Director, Mark Gale, recognized the importance of the Papal visit and the opportunity it presented the airport and the Philadelphia region. He recognized that airport staff had a demanding job to perform under stressful conditions, and that often they felt undervalued. He also recognized that the first and last interactions people have with the city are often at the airport, and that those interactions have a significant positive or negative impact on how a city is perceived.

For Philadelphia, that means a city that has too often been defined by past events that were more negative than positive. It was an unprecedented opportunity for updating perceptions. Philadelphia had gone through some tough times and rough years, but in 2015 the city was benefiting from an over decade-long renaissance. The Philadelphia of 2015 was a vastly different place than the Philadelphia of 1975, or '85, or '95 for that matter. Yet most people who aren't from the region, or haven't spent time in the region tend to have an image of Philadelphia that lacked updated information, so to speak. This was the airport's *ethos*, or credibility, issue.

Mark wanted to make sure all workers at PHL had the communication skills necessary to deliver an outstanding experience to those who passed through the airport, and for everyone to feel valued in the process.

He wanted to establish the credibility of Philadelphia in travelers' minds. He wanted to create positive emotions in the visitors by creating positive emotions in staff. And he wanted to deliver the message that Philadelphia was a world-class city worth visiting, and that airport workers could be a reflection of that.

Mark had one more challenge. Of the 20,000 workers at PHL, about 900 are employees of the airport and the other 19,000 work for various agencies, including the TSA, state and federal agencies, and the airlines themselves. He had direct authority over just 4% of the actual airport workforce even though he owned 100% of the responsibility for how the airport was perceived. So Mark had to be an exceptionally human communicator himself to get everyone to embrace his vision of exceptional human communication for airport visitors.

We sat down with Mark and his team to pinpoint his organization's Value Zones, so as to best target a communication skill-building program that would allow workers to become exceptionally human communicators and assure travelers felt positively about their interactions. This established the foundation for *pathos*, or emotion. We knew the interactions between terminal personnel and passengers were important, but equally important were the interactions between management and those same personnel. As a result, we knew our work would have to be far-reaching to have the impact we both desired, and include management as well as staff.

So what did we do? We put into action the three elements of exceptionally human communications. We knew we needed to approach people from multiple agencies, who very often do not work together, and get them on the same page to create a similar value experience for all the travelers the airport serves. To do this, we needed to establish our credibility and trust. And to do that, we decided it was first necessary to make sure that everyone attending these hospitality programs knew they were valued.

We began each program by listening. We asked participants to introduce themselves, let us know some additional personal information such as where they were born, and how long they've worked at the airport. We wanted them to know that we sought to know them as people first. Not only did we get a better sense of them, they got a better sense of each other, because these people worked at different agencies and often did not know the first thing about each other. Trust was being developed on all fronts. We wanted them to listen to each other as well, to recognize the years of experience in the room, and begin to forge relationships that would serve as the model for how they would interact with passengers.

This served as a foreshadowing of the listening

work that would come later. We also wanted to let them know how important they were to Mark and his executive team at PHL, and that he wanted to supply them with the skills needed to help them best take care of themselves during this stressful time. We wanted them to feel cared for, to feel positive about their relationship with the airport. By stressing how this program was as much about helping them care for themselves as it was about caring for others, they began to feel valued, important, and significant.

As they say on the airplane during the safety announcement, put your oxygen mask on first before assisting others, and this is in essence what we were doing for them, putting them first. We were clear with them about the challenge of their position, the stresses they were under, and that they would probably see no financial reward when things went well, and how they usually are blamed when things go wrong. We had an open and honest conversation about all this, helping to build the trust and set the tone for the work ahead. We listened, we empathized, and we were conscious to be exceptionally human with them, to employ the three elements. We let them know what skills they needed to develop and why. We gave them a reason and rationale for doing so in order to provide the *logos*, or the logic.

The most important question that needed to be addressed was motivation. How were we going to get these employees motivated to develop the skills needed without having any true incentives to offer? Without addressing this question first, the entire training program would ultimately end as a failure. So, we empathized. We let them speak of their experiences, of the difficulties of dealing with stressed-out people all the time, of the misplaced anger, frustration, and at times aggressive behavior they are subject to every day. We made certain that through our communication, by listening, by providing 100% of our attention, that they felt we were feeling what they were feeling. We made it clear that nobody expected them to suddenly change how they have been doing things; no one was asking them to make a 180-degree turn.

Instead, we gave them the 5% rule, that if they practiced being exceptionally human communicators 5% more often than they currently do, what would it look like for them. And it was essential to let them know that there are indeed many times when they are exceptional. And that was key, keeping it focused on them, and how the results would benefit them. Because if we kept focusing on the passengers, then we ran the risk of having some of the most essential perception-altering personnel feel overlooked, uncared for, and isolated. So it had to be about them. And if they felt cared for, respected, and understood, it significantly increased the chances they would do that for the passengers they dealt with every day. We built the credibility, we had them feeling positive about our interactions with them, and we pointed them in the right direction. Aristotle's three elements were put into action.

We know there would be no simple way to measure the direct impact this program would have. But Mark knew the status quo would not be enough, so he took a well thought out leap of faith. He knew that if the airport's workforce would consciously practice being exceptionally human 5% more often, it would be well worth it, as a 5% increase in customer satisfaction scores significantly impacts how an organization functions as well as how it is perceived. And by embarking on this effort, the airport received significant local press coverage highlighting these efforts. That in and of itself provided some direct, positive, and unexpected feedback as to the positive impact this would have. In making the commitment, the ball started rolling.

Many people who came to Philadelphia for the Pope expressed happiness with their visit, experiences for which the airport can claim its reasonable fair share. And many people working at the airport told Mark Gale his work had made a difference to them – and that the effort carried over to their interactions with airport visitors.

A Thought on Change:
It's Easier Than You Think!

As humans, we are creatures of habit. We're less inclined to change because change can be scary. Change means things *are* going to be different. Change requires concerted effort. And, perhaps most of all, change can be uncomfortable. And being uncomfortable, feeling discomfort, and perhaps a little pain, presents us with a challenge. Often any sign of discomfort or pain is seen as a problem, that something is wrong, and sends a signal that we should stop what we are doing so as to not make the discomfort worse. But there is a difference between good discomfort and bad discomfort.

Good discomfort is signaled by those sensations you feel the day after you start a new exercise routine. That soreness in your muscles that cause you to ache in ways you never thought you could ache before. There was a day, back in high school, where I felt like I couldn't move after the first day of wrestling practice. If we take that discomfort as a signal to stop doing what we're doing, then we'll never get into the physical shape we desire. The same thing goes with learning to play guitar. Your fingertips will ache until you eventually build up calluses, at which point the pain ceases. But if you don't go through that discomfort, you'll never learn to play guitar. On the other hand, the same activity can cause the bad discomfort: if after first working out, you feel a knife-like pain in your knee every step you take, then you may want to stop what you are doing and consider calling a doctor. That's the bad discomfort.

So, as you begin navigating the road towards becoming an exceptionally human communicator, and discomfort rears its uncomfortable head, ask yourself if this is something that I simply need to endure, or is this actively causing me harm? At times the answer may be apparent, and other times you may need to take some additional time and acquire more evidence before making that decision. One way or the other, you will feel some level of discomfort, so don't be surprised by it, simply embrace it. Easier said than done, I know, yet that perseverance and your effort, is well worth it.

Parting Thoughts

While every interaction matters, we are human and our ability to be exceptionally human has its limits. However, if we can intelligently pick the times we are exceptionally human, then our communication's impact can be equally exceptional. What I love about Aristotle and his rhetorical proofs, the three elements, is how they provide us with time-tested guidelines from which to build our communication practice. Practice is the key. Being exceptionally human requires practice, diligence, risk, failure, rewards, and discomfort. As we work to build new communication habits, habits that may require adjustment mid-flight, we develop the adaptability needed to

> *Being exceptionally human requires practice, diligence, risk, failure, rewards, and discomfort.*

become competent communicators. And what instills trust in one person will not necessarily do so in another, and what makes someone cry may make another laugh or remain indifferent.

Remember the Hollywood I spoke of in the first chapter, where I was born and raised, where Aristotle's three elements, *ethos*, *pathos*, and *logos*, were masterfully applied? The magic of the entertainment industry is that everything is staged, every detail is thought out well in advance, and every emotion expressed is carefully and meticulously trained for, so that as audience members, we believe, we feel, and we buy. If life could be that neatly presented, that well thought out in advance, then it would be a much different experience. Although it's not, that doesn't mean we cannot apply those same principles, those same techniques, when we are aware of the need to do so.

It's a test and an experiment, and only your continued efforts will prove what works best under what circumstances. It's a wondrous journey whose destinations can bring inspired rewards, and one that I urge you to take. So, next time you prepare to have a value-latent conversation, send that email, or post on social media, consider *ethos*, *pathos*, and *logos*, or credibility, emotion, and logic. And realize that being exceptionally human with one or two elements can help overshadow or compensate for simply being human with the other(s). Strong credibility can compensate for slightly flawed logic, as generating strong positive emotions combined with compelling arguments can boost credibility. Make sure you are listening and empathizing, and see what transpires. You'll be that much more effective with your communication, the results will be that much more powerfully positive, and you'll be that much more exceptionally human!

Exceptionally Human

Communication Skills Appendix

There are three key skills to help us become even more exceptionally human communicators. Here they are...

Listening

Chances are, in the course of your education, no matter the level completed, we all had to take math, English, science, and some type of history class. Chances are also high that we never took a class called listening. Now it's quite possible that listening was incorporated into another class, but that's not the same as having a class dedicated entirely to listening. I can tell you from my experience teaching classes in 19 different colleges and universities across the United States in Communication Studies, a field dedicated to researching the how and why of human communication, only one school offered a class called "Listening" (that was Cabrillo College in Aptos, California). Think about that for a minute. Of the vital skills we develop in our lives, listening has to rank up there in the top 3. And for some reason, nobody bothered to teach us how to do it. So, as a result, we learn on the fly, which usually is good enough, but good enough will not take us to great. And if we are in any way going to become the exceptionally human communicators we want to be, we need to begin by becoming better listeners.

Listening is a skill, and like any skill, be it playing a musical instrument, cooking, swimming, or dancing, we need to learn how to do it properly followed by practice, practice, practice. One of the reasons we haven't been taught how to listen is because if our ears function properly, if we can hear, then the assumption is that we are listening. Well, that's like saying just because we can press down the keys on a piano we are a pianist. The two are distinctly different things, as one is something that requires little effort and the other requires hours of dedicated practice to master. This is not to say we all need to now dedicate endless hours to develop our listening prowess, although it would be helpful, but this is about truly recognizing the distinctions between hearing and listening so we will know what we need to actually do to develop this vital skill.

First thing to recognize is that hearing is an involuntary response to stimuli, whereas listening is an active exercise in engagement. Hearing is effortless. We do not need to expend excessive energy to hear. If you've ever tried to go to sleep while traffic is roaring outside your window, you can attest to the fact that hearing happens, like it or not. Listening, however, requires effort, as effective listening involves more than simply **hearing**, it also involves **attending, understanding, responding,** and **remembering**. These five things constitute listening.

We've already covered hearing. **Attending** is actually paying attention to what is being communicated, being present and focused on what is being communicated as well as how it is being communicated. That means avoiding distractions and staying present with the other person, an increasingly difficult task in our on-demand age. **Understanding** is just that, making sure that what was communicated is something we understand, and if we don't understand it, we let the other person know so they can help achieve understanding. Don't nod in agreement or say you understand if you don't, because when you do you've technically stopped listening. **Responding** is providing the person who is communicating with us a sign that we are actually present with them. Whether a nodding head, a smile, or an emoji, it lets the other person know we are there with them. Finally, to truly have fully listened, we need to be able to recall what the other person has communicated; we need to **remember**. Now, we're not going to remember all things at all times, as we are human, but to be that *exceptionally human* listener, we need to take steps necessary to assure we can remember, like taking notes. It's only when we've heard, attended, understood, responded, and remembered, that we can say we have listened. Like I said, no simple task, but certainly one worth investing our time and energy to develop.

It's worth pointing out that there are very legitimate barriers to effective listening. I've already touched upon the fact we haven't been taught to listen. Other barriers include information overload, being distracted, not feeling well, competing thoughts, and fatigue are but a few. Simply recognize that we're not going to wake up tomorrow and magically become listening superstars. We need to make a concerted effort to listen, to block out distractions and dedicate ourselves to doing the 5 things required to listen. That's why I like the 5% rule. We're not going to be that exceptionally human listener all the time, but if we can make that concerted effort 5% more often, 24 more minutes than we do now, then we won't be putting too much pressure on ourselves and we'll go a long way in that direction.

So, why does listening matter? Because so few people have actually been taught how to listen, so few people do it well. And by becoming a better listener, you will stand out and be noticed. People like being listened to (they may actually be taken aback because it is so unusual). Listening enables us to find the deeper meaning behind the words people use, which is 90% or more of what constitutes communication. Listening allows us to develop strong connections with the people we communicate with, as people value people who listen to them. Listening builds that vital trust, increases your credibility, and people feel positively about their exchanges with us. Listening provides us with the insights that allow us to understand what others find rational, logical, and reasonable. Listening provides us with the insights that allow us to be a more competent communicator.

Empathy

What is empathy? Ask this question to someone on the street or at work and the answer might be understanding or knowing what someone else is feeling. And with that answer, you'll be halfway to empathy. The other, and even more important half, would include feeling what someone else is feeling. As a matter of fact, you could even dispose of the first half and simply define empathy as feeling what another person is feeling. That is what empathy truly is. And what's nice, is that as human beings, we are hard-wired to empathize, and at times it's an almost reflexive act. When you watch someone giving a presentation and it's clear from their delivery that they are extremely nervous, you start to feel nervous as well. That's because you are empathizing with them, feeling what they are feeling. When you watch movies, you get into the characters' emotions, and that's also the power of empathy (thanks to those mirror neurons in our brains). There are notable exceptions, such as people with narcissistic personality disorder or sociopaths, but for a vast majority of people, empathy is as natural as breathing.

But just because it's natural, doesn't mean that we always do it, and that in fact, there are countless other times when empathy requires tremendous focused effort. We can be so overcome by our own experiences, our own feelings, by stress and fatigue, that our ability to empathize becomes significantly compromised.

One significant challenge to empathy is taking our own emotional experience and placing it second, and placing the other person's emotional state first. Empathy demands that we put aside whatever it is we may be feeling so we can feel what another person is feeling. And that's no simple task, especially when we are experiencing rather charged emotions, such as anger, disappointment, or fear, as they tend to take us over completely. However, when we can move beyond what we are feeling, we can make the effort to, however briefly, step outside ourselves, we can gain valuable insights into the other person, insights that will inform the choices we make when we communicate with them in order to better connect with them. When we feel what someone else is feeling, and we are being exceptionally human communicators, other people will notice, because in this stress filled, rapidly changing, iWorld we live in, empathy has taken a back seat. More often than not, people are empathizing less often, through no fault of their own. Fortunately, with a

> *When we feel what someone else is feeling, and we are being exceptionally human communicators, other people will notice...*

little effort, it need not remain that way, and that is being exceptionally human.

Breathing

Modern life is stressful and stress has a significant impact on our thinking and communication behaviors. Typically when under stress, our brains will go into fight or flight mode; we will either confront the stress with aggression or hostility, or we will move away from or avoid the situation. Our breathing gets shallow as our bodies prepare to defend/attack or flee, and our capacity to engage in more meaningful communication practices becomes compromised, as blood is diverted from our brains and redistributed to other vital body organs. Our bodies seem to be hard-wired to have these stress responses, and although helpful in truly life-threatening situations, they can have significant down-sides in terms of our communication and the negative impact it has on others. We must find a way to work with stress so it does not work against us.

What is interesting is that when we are under physical stress, such as running or biking, our bodies respond in ways that allow us to overcome the stress in a positive manner. Our muscles are working harder, and as a result need additional oxygen. The way our muscles acquire oxygen is through the blood, so our breathing unconsciously deepens, more air enters our lungs, more oxygen enters our bloodstream, and feeds our stressed muscles. Perfect.

When we are under mental stress, however, our bodies respond in a way that makes it more difficult to overcome the stress in a positive manner. Our brains are working harder, and as a result, need additional oxygen. But instead of our breath deepening, our breathing becomes much more shallow, and we are in effect denying our bodies the one thing it needs to work more effectively, oxygen. As a result, our decision making capacity becomes compromised as the fight or flight response tightens its grip. To counteract this tendency, and to bring more blood flow and oxygen to our brains, we need to become conscious of our breathing.

I would like to focus on two types of breathing we engage in. The first is called **thoracic breathing**. Thoracic breathing is the shallow breathing we use almost all day long. We are drawing air into our lungs via our mouths, and as a result tend to only use the top 10% of our lung capacity, bringing in just enough oxygen so all systems are functioning well. And when we are under stress, our thoracic breathing, which is already shallow to begin with, gets that much more shallow. As a result, we are bringing less oxygen into our lungs, which means less oxygen into our blood, which means less oxygen into our brain.

Diaphragmatic breathing, on the other hand, is a deeper breathing practice that starts at the diaphragm, which lies just below our lungs. This breathing is best accessed via our nose, and we draw air much deeper into our lungs, almost like filling up a glass of water from the bottom to the top. As a result, we bring much more oxygen into our lungs, that gets transferred into our blood, and distributed to our brain and other vital organs. Whereas thoracic breathing requires little conscious effort, diaphragmatic breathing requires focused effort.

So, here's a simple diaphragmatic breathing exercise you can practice when stressful circumstances arise, you will be prepared to bring the much needed oxygen to your brain, so our exceptionally human communication practices can thrive.

1. Sit upright in your chair, spine straight, feet flat on the ground, hands resting comfortably on your thighs, eyes open.

2. Slowly exhale completely through your mouth, making sure your keep your spine straight.

3. Slowly, to a count of 5, gently inhale through you nose, engaging your diaphragm as you fill your lungs up with air from the bottom up to the to, like a glass being filled with water. (Note how your chest will rise as you do this.)

4. Once your lungs are full, hold for ½ second, then slowly and gently exhale to a count of 5, either through your nose or mouth, being certain to keep your spine straight so as to avoid collaps-ing your chest. (Note this is not a rapid exhale, but a controlled exhale.)

5. Once you've exhaled completely, inhale again (step 3), then exhale (step 4).

6. Repeat 5 times in a row, 2-3 times a day, for 3 weeks.

References

Bogart, Anne. *A Director Prepares*. New York, NY: Routledge, 2001.

Burleson, Brant and Caplan, Scott. "Cognitive Complexity." *Communication and Personality: Trait Perspectives*. 1998.

Cooper, Lane. *The Rhetoric of Aristotle*. London: Prentince Hall, 1932.

Ellis, Albert. *Overcoming Destructive Beliefs, Feelings, and Behaviors: New Directions for Rational Emotive Behavior Therapy*. Amherst, New York: Prometheus, 2001.

Gottman, Julie Schwartz and Gottman, John. "Lessons from the Love Lab." *Psychotherapy Networker*, November/December, 2015.

Hill, L., Brandeau, G., Truelove, E. and Lineback, K. *Collective Genius: The Art of Practice and Leading Innovation*. Boston: Harvard Business Review Press, 2014.

Littlejohn, Stephen W. *Theories of Human Communication*. Belmont, CA: Wadsworth, 1999.

Nayar, Vineet. *Employess First, Customers Second.* Boston: Harvard Business Press, 2010.

O'Connor, Malachi and Dornfeld, Barry. *The Moment You Can't Ignore.* New York NY: Public Affairs, 2014.

Pennebaker, James. *The Secret Life of Pronouns: What Our Words Say About Us.* New York: Bloomsbury, 2011.

Spitzberg, Brian H., and William R. Cupach. *Interpersonal communication competence.* Vol. 4. SAGE Publications, Incorporated, 1984.

Other Resources

Hurst, Arron. *The Purpose Economy.* Boise, ID: Elevate, 2014.

Moon, Youngme. *Different: Escaping the Competitive Herd.* New York: Crown Business, 2010.

Pink, Daniel H. *Drive: The Surprising Truth About What Motivates Us.* New York: Penguin, 2009.

Winner, Micehell Garcia and Crooke, Pamela. *Social Thinking at Work: Why Should I Care?* San Jose, CA: Think Social Publishing, 2011.

About the Author

Brian Shapiro is a dynamic professional, educator, and performing artist with over 20 years' experience in communication consulting, professional training, higher education, and the performing arts. He's a knowledgeable, insightful, and thoughtful communication consultant and trainer and is the founder and president of Shapiro Communications, a full-service communication consulting practice that partners with clients to develop and deliver communication skills programs with an artistic bent.

Brian is a lecturer at the University of Pennsylvania's Organizational Dynamics program and has taught an extensive array of Communication Studies courses at colleges throughout the U.S. Active in the performing arts, he has written and performed over 20 original performance art works nationally and internationally, and is the singer/songwriter for the Paris based electronic music trio, Grand Plateau.

Brian attended a doctorate program in Performance Studies at the University of Texas at Austin, and holds both a BA (San Diego State University) and MA (San Francisco State University) in Communication Studies. An avid yoga and tai chi practitioner, passionate music lover, vinyl collector, skier, bicycle commuter, all around arts and sports fan who's originally from Los Angeles, Brian and his family currently live in reinvigorated Philadelphia, PA, where he's learned the true meaning of the word seasons.

About Shapiro Communications

Shapiro Communications is in the satisfaction business, as we humanize organizational communication. Be it clients, customers, employees, or staff, we ensure your organization produces an unparalleled level of exemplary communication! Drawing upon the three pillars of exceptional communication, trust, emotions, and reason, we develop the skills required for customer + client experiences, exceptional employee performance, and increased organizational satisfaction.

Shapiro Communications serves a diverse client-base across multiple industries, including: Hospitality, Travel, Hi-Tech, Legal, Fortune 500, B2B, B2C, Non-profit, Governmental, Financial, Higher Education, and more. We take great pride in producing exceptionally positive results for all our clients.

Founded in San Francisco in 2010, Shapiro Communications is currently headquartered in Philadelphia, PA and provides an extensive suite of organizational communication services to the regional, national and international communities. All of our services are guaranteed and backed by the experience and expertise that the Shapiro Communications' team provides so that your organization's communication is exceptionally human.

For more information about Shapiro Communications, visit our website, **www.shapirocommunications.com**, or contact us via phone at 215.805.1695 or by email at **info@shapirocommunications.com**, or at 245 S. 16th Street, Philadelphia, PA 19102.

Also, check out our invaluable feedback tool: *Exceptionally Human Communication Profile.* Our original on-line service provides you with direct insights into how others perceive your communication in terms of credibility, emotions, and reason. To give it a try, or for more information, visit:

www.exceptionallyhuman.com

or

www.shapirocommunications.com

Exceptionally Human

Made in the USA
Charleston, SC
13 February 2017